Welcoming the Unwelcome

BOOKS BY PEMA CHÖDRÖN

Awakening Loving-Kindness

Becoming Bodhisattvas

Comfortable with Uncertainty

The Compassion Book

Living Beautifully

The Places That Scare You

The Pocket Pema Chödrön

Practicing Peace

Start Where You Are

Taking the Leap

When Things Fall Apart

The Wisdom of No Escape

WELCOMING *the* UNWELCOME

Wholehearted Living in a Brokenhearted World

PEMA CHÖDRÖN

SHAMBHALA
Boulder · 2019

Shambhala Publications, Inc.
4720 Walnut Street
Boulder, Colorado 80301
www.shambhala.com

9 8 7 6 5 4 3 2 1

FIRST EDITION
Printed in the United States of America

♾ This edition is printed on acid-free paper that meets the
American National Standards Institute z39.48 Standard.
♻ This book is printed on 30% postconsumer recycled paper.
For more information please visit www.shambhala.com.
Shambhala Publications is distributed worldwide by
Penguin Random House, Inc., and its subsidiaries.

Designed by Steve Dyer

LIBRARY OF CONGRESS CATALOGING-IN-PUBLICATION DATA
Names: Chödrön, Pema, author.
Title: Welcoming the unwelcome: wholehearted living in a
brokenhearted world / Pema Chödrön.
Description: First Edition. | Boulder: Shambhala, 2019.
Identifiers: LCCN 2018059669 | ISBN 9781611805659 (pbk.: alk. paper)
Subjects: LCSH: Spiritual life—Buddhism. | Bodhicitta (Buddhism)
Classification: LCC BQ7805.C494 2019 | DDC 294.3/444—dc23
LC record available at https://lccn.loc.gov/2018059669

This book is dedicated to

KHENCHEN THRANGU RINPOCHE

with love, devotion, and gratitude
for all his support and kindness
to me over many years.

CONTENTS

1. Begin with a Broken Heart   1

2. Does It Matter?   11

3. Overcoming Polarization   20

4. The Fine Art of Failure   30

5. The Path of Non-Rejecting   35

6. Just as It Is   42

7. How Not to Lose Heart   48

8. Beyond the Comfort Zone   57

9. Speaking from Our Shared Humanity   66

10. How You Label It Is How It Appears   73

11. The Practice of Open Awareness   81

12. Life Changes in an Instant   87

13. Cool Emptiness   95

14. Experiencing Nowness   100

15. Birth and Death in Every Moment   106

16. Imagine Life without Ego   112

17. Our Wisdom Changes the World   118

Contents

18. Welcoming the Unwelcome with Laughter   124

19. Learning from Our Teachers   129

20. Mission Impossible   139

PRACTICES FOR WELCOMING THE UNWELCOME   149

     Basic Sitting Meditation   151

     Tonglen Practice   154

     Locate, Embrace, Stop, Remain.   161

Acknowledgments   165

About the Author   167

Welcoming the Unwelcome

Begin with a Broken Heart

*Our aim is to fully awaken our heart and mind, not
just for our own greater well-being but also to bring
benefit, solace, and wisdom to other living beings.
What motivation could top that?*

WHEN YOU ENGAGE WITH SPIRITUAL TEACHINGS,
it is wise to know your intentions. For example, you
may ask yourself, "What is my purpose in reading this new
book, with its ominous title *Welcoming the Unwelcome*?" Are
you reading it because times are uncertain and you want
some clues about what will help you make it through whatever's coming? Are you reading it to gain wisdom about yourself? Do you hope it will help you get over certain emotional
or mental patterns that undermine your well-being? Or did
someone give it to you—with lots of enthusiasm—and now
you don't want to upset them by not reading it?

Your motivation may include some or all of the above.
They are all good reasons (even the last one) for reading
this or any book. But in the Mahayana Buddhist tradition to
which I belong, when studying spiritual teachings, we set out

by arousing an even greater motivation, known as *bodhichitta*. In Sanskrit, *bodhi* means "awake" and *chitta* means "heart" or "mind." Our aim is to fully awaken our heart and mind, not just for our own greater well-being but also to bring benefit, solace, and wisdom to other living beings. What motivation could top that?

The Buddha taught that all of us, at our essence, are good and loving. Because of this basic goodness, we naturally want to be there for others, especially those who are closest to us and those who are in the greatest need. We are keenly aware that others need us, and that our society and the planet as a whole need us, especially now. We want to do what we can to alleviate the fear, anger, and painful groundlessness that so many of us are experiencing these days. But what often happens when we try to help is that we find our own confusion and habitual tendencies getting in the way. I hear people talking like this: "I wanted to help at-risk teenagers, so I studied and trained, and I went into social work. Two days into the job, I found myself hating most of the kids! My initial feeling was 'Why can't we just get rid of all these kids and find some nicer ones who will cooperate with me?' It was then that I realized I had to clean up my own act first."

Bodhichitta, the awakened heart, begins with the wish to be free from whatever gets in the way of our helping others. We long to be free from the confused thoughts and habitual patterns that cover up our basic goodness, so that we can be less reactive, less fearful, and less stuck in our old ways. We understand that to whatever degree we can get beyond our neuroses and habits, we can be more available for those teenagers, for our family members, for our larger community, or for the strangers we meet. We may still be going through strong feelings and reactions on the inside, but if we know how to work with these emotions without falling into our usual ruts, then we can be right there for others. And even if there's nothing dramatic we can do to help, other people will feel our support, which actually helps a lot.

Bodhichitta begins with this aspiration, but it doesn't stop there. Bodhichitta is also a commitment. We commit to doing all it takes to free ourselves completely from all our varieties of confusion and unconscious habit and suffering, because these prevent us from being fully there for others. In the language of Buddhism, our ultimate commitment is to attain "enlightenment." In essence, this means knowing fully who we really are. When we are enlightened, we will be fully awake to our deepest nature, which is fundamentally open-hearted, open-minded, and available for others. We will know this to be true beyond any doubt, beyond any going back. In this state, we will possess the greatest possible wisdom and skill with which we can benefit others and help them to awaken completely themselves.

To fulfill the commitment of bodhichitta, we will need to learn everything there is to learn about our own heart and mind. This is a big job. It will most likely include reading books, listening to teachings, and deeply contemplating what we study. We will also learn a great deal about ourselves by having a regular practice of basic sitting meditation. In the back of the book I've included a simple meditation technique you can use anywhere. Finally, we will have to test and clarify our growing knowledge by applying it to our own lives, to the situations we naturally find ourselves in. When bodhichitta becomes the basis for how we live each day of our lives, then everything we do is meaningful. Our existence feels incredibly rich. This is why it makes so much sense to bring to mind bodhichitta as often as possible.

Sometimes the wonderful motivation of bodhichitta arises easily. But when we're feeling anxious or self-concerned, when our confidence level is low, bodhichitta can seem beyond our reach. In such times, how can we uplift our hearts to generate the courageous longing to wake up for the benefit of others? How can we intentionally turn our mind around when it is feeling small?

My root teacher Chögyam Trungpa Rinpoche taught me a method for transforming the mind that I still follow. The first thing to do is to bring to mind a poignant image or story, something that naturally warms up your heart and puts you in touch with the human predicament. Maybe someone you really care about has recently been diagnosed with cancer or a degenerative disease. Or someone you care about with drug or alcohol problems, who has been doing well for a long time, has just relapsed. Or perhaps your dear friend has suffered a great loss. Maybe you saw something sad when you went to the grocery store, such as a painful interaction between a parent and a child. Or you think about the homeless woman you always see on the way to work. Or maybe you were affected by something you read in the news, such as a story about a famine or a family being deported.

Trungpa Rinpoche said that the way to arouse bodhichitta was to "begin with a broken heart." Protecting ourselves from pain—our own and that of others—has never worked. Everybody wants to be free from their suffering, but the majority of us go about it in ways that only make things worse. Shielding ourselves from the vulnerability of all living beings—which includes our own vulnerability—cuts us off from the full experience of life. Our world shrinks. When our main goals are to gain comfort and avoid discomfort, we begin to feel disconnected from, and even threatened by, others. We enclose ourselves in a mesh of fear. And when many people and countries engage in this kind of approach, the result is a messy global situation with lots of pain and conflict.

Putting so much effort into protecting our hearts from pain hurts us over and over again. Even when we realize it's unhelpful, this is a hard habit to break. It's a natural human tendency. But when we generate bodhichitta, we go against the grain of this tendency. Instead of shying away, we arouse the bravery to take a direct look at ourselves and the world. Instead of being intimidated by phenomena, we come to embrace all aspects of our inexhaustibly rich lives.

We can touch in with bodhichitta by simply allowing ourselves to experience our own raw feelings, without getting sucked into our thoughts and stories about them. For instance, when I'm feeling lonely, I can blame myself, or I can fantasize about how nice it would be to have someone to spend time with. But I also have the opportunity to simply touch into that lonely feeling and discover bodhichitta is right there, in my own vulnerable heart. I can realize that my own loneliness is no different from the loneliness everyone else on this planet experiences. Similarly, my unwanted feelings about being left out or unjustly accused can connect me to all those who are similarly suffering.

When I'm embarrassed, when I feel like a loser, when I feel that something is fundamentally wrong with me, bodhichitta is present in those emotions. When I've made a big mistake, when I've failed to do what I set out to do, when I feel the sting of having let everyone down—at such times

I have the option to tap into the awakened heart of bodhichitta. If I really connect with my jealousy, my anger, or my prejudice, I find myself standing in the shoes of humanity. From this place, the longing to wake up to alleviate the suffering of the world comes naturally.

There is a long history of people successfully uncovering their basic goodness and basic bravery through dedicated practice. Some are famous religious figures, but most are not widely known, such as my friend Jarvis Masters, who has been in a California prison for more than thirty years. We won't always feel inspired to follow their examples and go fearlessly against the grain. Our confidence will ebb and flow. And the teachings never tell us to bite off more than we can chew. But if we gradually increase our capacity to be present with our pain and the sufferings of the world, we will surprise ourselves with our growing sense of courage.

In our practice of cultivating a broken heart, we can incrementally build the strength and skill to handle more and more. Trungpa Rinpoche, who had a huge capacity for being in the presence of suffering without turning away, would often bring to mind a time in Tibet when he was about eight years old. He was on the roof of a monastery and saw a group of young boys stoning a puppy to death. Though they were quite far away, he could see the terrified eyes of the dog and hear the boys' laughter. They were doing it just for fun. Rinpoche wished he could do something to save the puppy, but he was helpless. For the rest of his life, all he had to do was recall that time, and a strong desire to alleviate suffering would arise in his heart. The memory of the dog gave his desire to wake up a sense of urgency. This is what propelled him, day after day, to make the best use of his life.

Most of us, one way or another, try to do good in the world. This is a natural result of our having basic goodness. But our positive motivations are often mixed with other factors. For example, some people try to be helpful because they feel bad about themselves. They hope to look good in the eyes of the world. Through their efforts, they hope to improve their standing with others, which may then raise their feeling of self-worth. Based on my long experience of living in communities, I can say that these people often accomplish an astonishing amount. You hear others saying, "Maria is worth six people," or "I wish everyone was like Jordan." In most ways, they're the ones you want on your team. But at the same time, they don't seem to get any closer to waking up. We all probably know someone who says things like, "I give and give and give and I never get thanked!" This kind of frustration is a sign that the underlying issues aren't being worked out.

Some people work hard, day and night, in the field of helping others, but their strongest motivation is to stay busy so they can avoid feeling their own pain. Some are driven by an idea of being "good," instilled in them by their family or culture. Some are motivated by feelings of obligation or guilt. Some do good to keep themselves out of trouble. Some are driven by the prospect of rewards, in this life or maybe in a future existence. Some are even motivated by resentment, anger, or a need to control.

If we take a good look within, we will probably discover that motivations like these are mixed with our genuine desire to help others. We shouldn't beat ourselves up about this because all these motivations come from our natural human tendency to look for happiness and to protect ourselves from pain. But they do keep us from becoming more connected with our own hearts and with the hearts of other people. This makes it difficult for us to benefit others in any deep way.

In contrast, the motivation of bodhichitta leads to more profound and long-lasting results because it's based on understanding where suffering comes from. At the outer level, there are the immense sufferings that we see and hear about and may experience from time to time—the cruelty, hunger, fear, abuse, and violence that plague people and animals and the planet itself. Every one of these comes from emotions such as greed and aggression, which in turn come from not understanding the basic goodness of our true nature. This ignorance is at the root of all our suffering. It lies beneath everything we do to harm ourselves and others. When we arouse bodhichitta, we commit to overcoming everything that obscures our innate wisdom and warm-heartedness, everything that cuts us off from our natural ability to empathize with and benefit others.

This awakening to our true nature doesn't happen overnight. And even as we begin to awaken and find ourselves more and more able to help others, we have to accept that there's not always something we can do—at least not immediately. Without making excuses or succumbing to indifference, we have to acknowledge that this is just how things are. Countless people and animals are suffering at this very moment, but how much can we do to prevent that? If we're on the roof of a monastery witnessing boys stone a puppy, maybe all we can do in the moment is to not turn away and to let the unfolding tragedy deepen our bodhichitta. Then we can let ourselves become curious about what causes people to hurt animals in the first place. Instead of seeing the boys' behavior as something alien to us, we can look for its roots within ourselves. Does the aggression or blindness that lies behind such actions dwell within our own heart? If we can find common ground in this way, then maybe the next time we encounter something similar, we'll be in a better position to communicate. And when we fully awaken to our true nature, we'll have a much greater ability to influence others. But even then, what we can do to help will be limited by circumstances.

So, when we arouse bodhichitta, it's important to understand that we're in it for the long haul. We will have to stick around for a long time and apply tremendous effort and patience. The supreme vision of bodhichitta is to help every single living being awaken to their true nature. Our only shot at accomplishing this is by first attaining enlightenment ourselves. Along the way, we can take one step at a time, doing our best to keep our longing and commitment going during the ups and downs of our lives.

As you read this book, please try to keep in mind the larger context of bodhichitta. This will be a lot more fruitful than reading it for intellectual stimulation. If you begin with a broken heart, a heart that longs to help others, then you may find a few things here to take away with you. Of all the words in this book, there might be one paragraph or one sentence—maybe one I didn't even realize was that important—that clicks for you in just the right way. Something may change the way you see things and actually move you closer to being able to alleviate suffering in the world.

These teachings are not just my own ideas. They are my attempt to communicate the wisdom I have received from my teachers, who received it from their teachers and so on, in a line of sages stretching back thousands of years. If you come to them with the motivation of bodhichitta, there is no limit to the benefit they can bring. When we're really in touch with the longing to help others, and when our lives are committed to that purpose, we can consider ourselves among the most fortunate people on this earth.

2

Does It Matter?

When we start to ask ourselves, "Does it matter?"
we realize how many aspects there are to every situation.
We begin to appreciate how interconnected we are to the
rest of the world, and how even our thought patterns
can lead to a whole series of consequences.

SOMETIMES WE CATCH OURSELVES ABOUT TO DO
something that doesn't quite feel right. We're about to
react habitually and we feel a tinge of misgiving or queasi-
ness. At such times, we may avoid a lot of trouble by asking
ourselves a simple question: Does it matter?

For instance, when I'm about to send a harsh or slanderous
email, does it matter? Does it matter to me? Does it matter to
others? When I'm about to take something that's not offered,
does it matter? Does it make any difference even if no one
finds out? When I eat the last piece, or throw the can out
the window, or glare at someone, does it matter? What are the
consequences of my behavior? Am I causing harm to myself
or others? If I go off on someone, does it matter? If I then
feel justified in doing so, does it matter? Does it matter if I

apologize? What drama will be set in motion by these words or this act? Will they have any larger impact on the world?

These questions are closely related to one of the Buddha's main interests: how to lead a virtuous life. Every spiritual tradition is concerned with virtue, but what does virtue mean? Is it the same as following a list of dos and don'ts? Does a virtuous person have to be a goody-goody? Is it necessary to be dogmatic, rigid, and smug? Or is there room to be playful, spontaneous, and relaxed? Is it possible to enjoy life while at the same time being virtuous?

Like many spiritual traditions, the Dharma has lists of positive and negative actions. Buddhists are encouraged to commit to some basic precepts, such as not to kill, steal, or lie. Members of the monastic community, such as myself, have much longer lists of rules to follow. But the Buddha didn't establish these rules merely for people to conform to outer codes of behavior. The Buddha's main concern was always to help people become free of suffering. With the understanding that our suffering originates from confusion in our mind, his objective was to help us wake up out of that confused state. He therefore encouraged or discouraged certain forms of behavior based on whether they promoted or hindered that process of awakening.

When we ask ourselves, "Does it matter?" we can first look at the outer, more obvious results of our actions. But then we can go deeper by examining how we are affecting our own mind: Am I making an old habit more habitual? Am I strengthening propensities I'd like to weaken? When I'm on the verge of lying to save face, or manipulating a situation to go my way, where will that lead? Am I going in the direction of becoming a more deceitful person or a more guilty, self-denigrating person? How about when I experiment with practicing patience or generosity? How are my actions affecting my process of awakening? Where will they lead?

By questioning ourselves in these ways, we start to see "virtue" in a new light. Virtuous behavior is not about doing "good" because we feel we're "bad" and need to shape up. Instead of guilt or dogma, how we choose to act can be guided by wisdom and kindness. Seen in this light, our question then boils down to "What awakens my heart, and what blocks that process from happening?"

In the language of Buddhism, we use the word "karma." This is a way of talking about the workings of cause and effect, action and reaction. Or, as some people like to put it, "What goes around comes around." It's said that if we want to learn about our past, we should look at our present circumstances, for they are the result of our past actions. If we want to learn about our future, we should look at what we're doing now. For me, the latter is the more helpful aspect of karma to think about. There's nothing we can do to change the past and the present, but the future is unwritten. What we do right now will help create that future—which is not just our own future, but a future we share with many others.

Every word we speak and every action we perform affects our future, but where do words and actions come from? They all start from our mind. When we indulge in resentment or obsession or self-righteous thinking, we create several problems for ourselves. First, we suffer the immediate pain of those thoughts and emotions. Then we often act out in ways that cause ourselves and others harm. Finally, we reinforce a habit that we would be better off without.

This last result is the most insidious one. In brain science there's a lot of talk these days about neuroplasticity. Our habits are like grooves in the brain, which get deeper and deeper as we follow our usual thought patterns. There's no way out of the habit as long as we keep following the same rut. But when we interrupt our habitual behavior or go against our propensities, we start to establish new pathways in the brain.

This scientific view is very similar to the Buddhist idea of karmic seeds. With our actions and thoughts, we are constantly sowing seeds in our unconscious that will eventually bear fruit when the right conditions come together. Say you visit your cousin Monique, with whom you have a history of feeling irritated. During much of your time together, your continual feeling of annoyance is reinforcing itself. This sows new seeds of irritation in your unconscious. Even if you don't throw a glass against the wall, or say something nasty, you "act out" in your thoughts—say by spending half an hour in bed pondering Monique's long list of shortcomings. Then you go home and don't see her for a while. Maybe you completely stop thinking about her. But the next time her name is mentioned, even five years later, you get irritated again—and again you reinforce that propensity. Whatever your reaction, it sows more seeds in your mind, which bear more fruit in the future, and so on.

This is an illustration of why cyclic habitual patterns are so difficult to escape. In this example, it may seem like not much is at stake. But what happens when you have this situation with someone you live with or work with, such as your child or your spouse or your boss? What happens when this is the situation between two countries? And even in the case of your rarely seen cousin Monique, there are broader repercussions. For example, your irritation may promote bad feelings or cause rifts within your family. It may reinforce your general habit of feeling easily annoyed. It may strengthen your pattern of taking things too personally, or focusing on other people's flaws, or not being able to see things from another person's point of view. When we start to ask ourselves, "Does it matter?" we realize how many aspects there are to every situation. We begin to appreciate how interconnected we are to the rest of the world, and how even our thought patterns can lead to a whole series of consequences.

Many of my teachers talk about the necessity of maintaining *payu*. This Tibetan word can be translated as "discernment," "heedfulness," "awareness," or "attentiveness." When we understand that there are repercussions to everything we do, say, and even think, we feel inspired to maintain our *payu* as much as possible. We won't immediately arrive at a state where our *payu* is so fine-tuned that nothing gets by us. But it's a big help to have an awareness of karmic consequences and a sense of what will make things better or worse. It keeps us from getting completely entangled in painful emotions such as aggression or greed. We may still feel angry or greedy, but *payu* prevents us from going all the way with those emotions, to the point where we're creating a huge mess. *Payu* makes us more intelligent about how we lead our life.

We never know what will happen next in our lives or what will arise next in our mind. Whatever we do leaves an imprint in our mind, which remains latent until the right circumstances come together—for instance, the next time we hear the name "Monique." Dzigar Kongtrul Rinpoche likens this to taking a photo with a Polaroid camera. When the film is exposed to light, the chemicals on the negative react and the picture becomes clear.

Recently I had an interesting experience along these lines. A feeling came over me that I hadn't had in many decades—a feeling of rejection, almost like being jilted. This was big for me as a teenager, when I felt that way constantly. I never had the right clothes or the right hair—basically, I didn't fit the job description of being a human being. But when that feeling came up again recently, I had no idea where it came from. It's not as if I've been jilted lately, but still that same lonely, abandoned feeling arose. It was completely irrational, yet for some unknown reason the right conditions had arrived for the developed Polaroid to appear. Unlike when I was a teenager, however, this experience had no power over me. This was because I could see it for what it was, instead of getting immersed in it and sowing more seeds of feeling rejected.

Though we can't predict or control what will come up next or how we will feel about it, we can do something about how we react. We can work on how we relate to whatever comes up. This is where "Does it matter?" comes in. The question implies that we always have a choice in how we respond. And the more we go through our days with *payu* in our minds, the more that choice will be accessible to us.

When unwelcome events occur in our lives, it's hard to break out of our habitual patterns. We tend to get completely hooked and proceed blindly, without any insight, which just perpetuates our habit. At other times, we're tempted to go after something we know will be bad for us—unhealthy behavior, an unhealthy relationship, unhealthy food—and the pull of our propensity is too strong. During any of these challenging situations, it's easy to think we're doomed to re-peat our patterns until the end of time.

However, we can look at this from a much more optimis-tic point of view. If our aim is to wake up for the benefit of ourselves and other living beings, then it's necessary for us to change. These challenging times give us the greatest op-portunity for change. Every time we catch ourselves going down the rut of a habitual reaction, we have a chance to in-terrupt the momentum and discover a whole new direction and depth to our life.

As Trungpa Rinpoche said, "Any experience can be made into a further blockage or can become a way of freeing our-selves." He gives the example of looking down and seeing a fly on your leg. If you have a tendency to feel aggressive toward flies, you could go with that feeling and *slap*—kill the fly. That becomes a means of further blockage; you sow more seeds of aggression and insensitivity, which hinder the process of awakening your heart. On the other hand, even if this goes against your tendency, you could try having a friendly response to the fly. You could just look at it in a kind way and either let it be there or gently put your hand near it so it will fly away. This transforms the fly's visit from an an-noying event into an opportunity for sowing seeds of kind-ness and tolerance and appreciating the sacredness of life. It turns into a small way of becoming more open-hearted and open-minded—in other words, of freeing yourself.

We're not doomed in any way because whatever happens, we can begin, right now, to do our very best. There's always something small we can do to alter our habitual response, even a little bit. It could be taking a few conscious breaths, or stepping back for a moment, or walking around the block to change the energy. It could be anything, as long as it interrupts the process of escalating our suffering in the exact same habitual way, over and over and over.

Overcoming our habits is not going to happen overnight. If you have a strong propensity to eat too much of a certain food, it's a little harsh to expect you'll stop eating it forever, starting today. What if you're in your office, trying to get some work done, and an overpowering smell of chocolate chip cookies wafts in through your window? (And chocolate chip cookies happen to be the exact food that you have the worst problem with overeating.) How do you handle the situation in a sane way? Do you have to close the window, go to the far corner of your room, and sit in the full lotus position until you think the smell has passed? That's not a realistic solution. On the other hand, you can also avoid the opposite extreme. You don't have to rush down the stairs immediately to get your hands on them. Simply take a moment or two to stay where you are and fully experience the feeling of craving those cookies. This small effort will do something to affect your habits. It will alter the pathways in your brain. Then, even if you go down and have some cookies, you can know that you've succeeded in slightly changing your pattern. If you keep applying this method, those changes will add up. Eventually the smell of chocolate chip cookies will not have the same overwhelming effect on your mind. But that doesn't mean you can't enjoy them.

It does indeed matter what we do, say, and even think. Everything counts, everything leaves an imprint in our minds. But at the same time, there's plenty of room for us to relax and appreciate what life has to offer. Asking "Does it matter?" and working with *payu* is a gentle, but effective,

method for working with our karma and gradually transforming our mind and its habits. If we get the hang of this
approach, we will find ourselves enjoying our lives more than
ever because we won't be continually dragged down by our
self-destructive propensities. This is why the Buddha encourages us to lead a virtuous life.

3

Overcoming Polarization

*The time we live in is a fertile ground for training
in being open-minded and open-hearted. If we can learn
to hold this falling apart–ness without polarizing and
without becoming fundamentalist, then whatever we do
today will have a positive effect on the future.*

THERE ARE MANY WAYS TO TALK ABOUT THE PROB-
lems of this world, but one way or another, all of them
have to do with polarization. We all have a tendency to divide
people, things, and ideas into sharply contrasting categories.
Consciously or unconsciously, we carry around concepts of
"us" and "them," "right" and "wrong," "worthy" and "unworthy." In this framework, there's not much room for a middle
ground; everything is at one pole or another. When groups
of people or whole nations get together around these concepts, they can become hugely magnified, which may result
in large-scale suffering: discrimination, oppression, war.

These national and global problems have their roots in
the subtle workings of our own individual minds. All of us,
to our own degree, experience some feeling of opposition

inside ourselves, with each other, and with the world around us. We're never quite satisfied with ourselves as we are, other people as they are, things as they are. Often, we feel this as an aversion to whatever we're experiencing. We don't like what's happening and we want to get rid of it. This can start out as a subtle level of aversion, which can grow into more obvious irritation. From there it may escalate into full-blown anger and hatred. Other times our feeling of opposition has to do with desire or craving. For instance, we may want an object or situation very badly because we think it will make us happy. But these desires are also based on seeing things as separate from us—seeing them as "other." In either case—aversion or desire—we're caught in some form of polarization. Whether we are "for" or "against," there is a lack of openness and relaxation in our minds. If we observe ourselves closely, we'll probably discover that this is the case much of the time.

Fortunately, there are effective ways of working with our tendency to polarize. We can begin by self-reflecting and noticing the "for" or "against" quality of our thoughts, words, and actions. We can also notice and take joy in those moments when we're not polarizing. Throughout the day we can ask ourselves: Am I perpetuating my sense of being in opposition? Or am I going against that tendency by lessening the gap between myself and the world? Am I increasing my sense of separateness from others? Or am I nurturing bodhichitta, the longing and commitment to wake up for the benefit of all living beings?

It's fairly straightforward to work with polarization on the level of physical action. For instance, if I turn on my shower and then discover a spider in the tub, I have two main options.

I can let the water run and leave the spider to its fate. This is a polarizing action because it creates a big gap between us. My aversion or indifference to the spider blinds me to what we have in common as living beings. Both of us want to be happy and not suffer; both of us want to live and not die. My other option is to turn off the water, get a piece of toilet paper, and use it to help the little fellow get out of danger. Then I can think, "The day's hardly begun and I've saved a life!" As Dzigar Kongtrul Rinpoche once said, "It may be a small event for you, but it's a major event for the spider." But in a sense, it can be a major event for me as well, because it nurtures my awakening heart. We can try to go through each day with a heightened awareness of our actions, taking every opportunity we find to lessen the gap.

Sometimes we will succeed, but other times we'll fail. We may even fail miserably. What happens then? Say you feel such a strong opposition to someone that you shove them or punch them—or worse. This kind of escalation can happen to anybody. When the perfect storm of frustrating conditions arises, you don't have to be a classically violent person to get out of control. What should you do then? What's the best way to turn away from your polarizing behavior and get back on the path of bodhichitta?

One popular method for dealing with these kinds of actions is to feel guilty. If what we did was especially aggressive or hurtful, this guilt could last a long time, maybe even for the rest of our life. But hiding out in a state of guilt won't help us overcome our feeling of separateness. It won't contribute at all to our waking up. So instead of reacting to what we did with guilt, we can make the best of the situation and use our unpleasant experience to get smarter.

If you shoved someone out of anger, you can start to turn things around by just acknowledging your harsh behavior. You can allow yourself to be openly aware that you've added aggression and strife to our planet—which you know doesn't need any more than it already has. You can feel regret for what you did, but it's important to do your best to bypass the heavy-handed guilt-tripping. Being conscious in this way, without beating yourself up, can be a huge departure from your previous patterns of protecting yourself from owning your negative behaviors by repressing or trying to ignore them. For at this moment, you have a chance to turn your mistake into something positive.

What you've just done makes you vividly aware of the painful reality that all over the world, every day, people are shoving each other, stabbing each other, shooting each other, being cruel to each other in many ways. This all happens out of ignorance—ignorance of our interconnectedness with each other and of our own basic goodness. But now, instead of beating yourself up for losing it, you can aspire to be more aware of your own hurtful actions, and more aware of how widespread these kinds of actions are in the world. Your action has opened your eyes to the human condition, to how fragile and vulnerable we all are. This heartbreaking thought makes you long to do whatever it takes to help. You understand from your experience how important it is to find a way to work with your habitual patterns, to learn how to stay present with your emotions without letting them escalate and spill out into action. You want to become fully conscious of how you get into that extreme, polarized place to begin with. This is how you naturally renew your commitment to wake up for the benefit of others. In this way, your seeming mistake can turn into a source of bodhichitta.

The idea is for us to become more and more aware of what we're doing, and more and more aware that our actions have consequences. Examining our behavior to see whether it's polarizing is an extension of the question "Does it matter?" Once we see what's at stake—not just for ourselves, but for our surrounding environment and for the planet as a whole, which suffers so much from polarization—we are naturally motivated to apply *payu*, heedfulness. We can gradually refine our *payu* so that it's present at more subtle levels of our behavior, beginning with our words.

I haven't shoved anyone in a long time, and I do whatever I can not to harm animals, even the peskiest insects and rodents—but speech is a whole different level of challenge. We can all appreciate how hard it is not to let harmful words slip out of our mouths. There are so many varieties of polarizing speech, from gross insults and lies, to subtle digs and other cutting remarks, to slander and gossip and all the other ways we have of creating divisions between people. Sometimes our polarizing speech is so familiar and so accepted among the people we hang out with that we're not even aware of the harm it may be causing. As with physical action, the method for overcoming polarizing speech is to become more aware of what we're doing—without getting into guilt—and to use our regrettable experience as a way of increasing bodhichitta.

Then we get to the subtlest level of polarization—the level of our mind. Unlike our actions and words, our thoughts don't go out into the world and have blatant repercussions. But are these thoughts really so unimportant? We're just sitting there, harmlessly thinking to ourselves, "She deserves to be taken down a peg. And what he did was definitely wrong. I know because I took a poll and everyone agrees with me." We may be sitting in a stream of critical, judgmental thoughts all day long and not realize how much polarization we're creating in our own mind. The grooves in our brain deepen with each repetitive thought and form habitual patterns, beliefs, and attitudes. Conscious or not, these patterns increase our propensity to separate ourselves from others, and subtly undermine our wish to awaken on their behalf. They also inevitably come out in our speech and actions. If you're constantly judging Isaiah in your mind, there's a good chance he'll eventually find out what you really think of him, and it won't be pretty. But if you never indulge in critical thoughts about Gabrielle, there's no chance you'll ever snap at her when you haven't slept enough. If we develop a healthy caution about the destructive power of our thoughts, we'll have much more incentive to nip our judgmental thinking in the bud. Then we'll be able to feel more at ease in all situations, especially when we're with people who push our buttons.

Polarization is at its most problematic when we dehumanize people—when we forget that the people we judge, criticize, and disagree with are actually as fully human as we are. This dehumanization can manifest in an obvious way, such as apartheid, slavery, police brutality, or genocide. But some level of this kind of prejudice exists in all of our minds. If we're honest with ourselves, we'll see that we habitually dehumanize others for many reasons. For instance, if people have political views that we consider narrow-minded or backward, we may have trouble seeing them as wholly human. If they don't believe in climate change or evolution, we may unconsciously disqualify them as fully developed members of the human race. We may condemn people for their behavior or criticize them because they smoke or drink or wear what we consider tacky clothes. Even such minor differences in our habits and preferences can cause us to feel fundamentally separate from others.

If we commit to being aware of our tendency to polarize, and we counteract that by arousing bodhichitta, we will gradually close these gaps. Then we'll be able to see all people as fellow human beings who want to be happy just like us. This covers not just climate change deniers and people who smoke, but even those who ruthlessly and callously bring suffering to others—such as perpetrators of hate crimes, greedy heads of corporations, sexual predators, and criminals who prey on the elderly.

There's a practice I like called "Just like me." You go to a public place and sit there and look around. Traffic jams are very good for this. You zero in on one person and say to yourself things such as "Just like me, this person doesn't want to feel uncomfortable. Just like me, this person loses it sometimes. Just like me, this person doesn't want to be disliked. Just like me, this person wants to have friends and intimacy."

We can't presume to know exactly what someone else is feeling and thinking, but still we do know a lot about each other. We know that people want to be cared about and don't want to be hated. We know that most of us are hard on ourselves, that we often get emotionally triggered, but that we want to be of help in some way. We know that, at the most basic level, every living being desires happiness and doesn't want to suffer.

If we view others from the standpoint of "Just like me," we have a strong basis to connect with them, even in situations where it seems most natural and reasonable to polarize. Even when extreme religious groups behead people or a racist gunman murders people praying in church, there is room to feel our connection with the perpetrators rather than dehumanize them.

The mother of James Foley, one of the journalists beheaded by ISIS, said of her son's executioner, "We need to forgive him for not having a clue what he was doing." This level of compassion can only happen when we have a sense of the complexity of what makes people reach the point of committing such crimes. Those who believe in violence are desperate to get some kind of ground under their feet, desperate to get away from their unpleasant feelings, desperate to be the one who's right. What would we do if we felt so desperate?

Having compassion for those who have harmed us—and especially those who have taken away our loved ones—doesn't come easily. We shouldn't feel like there's something wrong with us if we don't at present feel this degree of understanding and caring. In fact, it's quite exceptional to feel this way. As a precursor to this level of empathy, sorrow—simple sorrow— is often more accessible. For instance, in this case of the violence committed by extreme militants, we can tap into a deep sorrow for the situation as a whole. Along with our sorrow for the victims, we can also feel sorrow that young men find themselves hating so much, sorrow that they're stuck in such a pattern of hatred. Since things have such complex and far-reaching causes, we can feel sorrow for the circumstances where ignorance or suffering in the past created the hatred that is manifesting in these young men now. We can harness this all-encompassing sorrow to arouse the broken-hearted feeling that fosters bodhichitta.

Having compassion doesn't mean we can't take a stand. It's important to speak up when we've been hurt, when we see others being hurt, and when we observe or experience examples of abuse of power. It is equally important to listen deeply and without judgment when people speak about their experiences and their suffering. What has been dysfunctional does need to be openly addressed.

We are at a time when old systems and ideas are being questioned and falling apart, and there is a great opportunity for something fresh to emerge. I have no idea what that will look like and no preconceptions about how things should turn out, but I do have a strong sense that the time we live in is a fertile ground for training in being open-minded and open-hearted. If we can learn to hold this falling apart–ness without polarizing and without becoming fundamentalist, then whatever we do today will have a positive effect on the future.

Working with polarization and dehumanization won't put an immediate end to the ignorance, violence, and hatred that plague this world. But every time we catch ourselves polarizing with our thoughts, words, or actions, and every time we do something to close that gap, we're injecting a little bodhichitta into our usual patterns. We're deepening our appreciation for our interconnectedness with all others. We're empowering healing, rather than standing in its way. And because of this interconnectedness, when we change our own patterns, we help change the patterns of our culture as a whole. The results won't be immediately apparent. You probably won't notice any big changes in just a week or even a year. But please don't give up too easily and think, "This bodhichitta doesn't work for me. I'm going to look for something where the results are more immediate and tangible." Believe me when I say your patience will pay off. If you commit to overcoming polarization in your own mind, it's a life changer, and it will help the world as well.

4

The Fine Art of Failure

*If we can go beyond blame and other escapes
and just feel the bleeding, raw meat quality of
our vulnerability, we can enter a space where
the best part of us comes out.*

OUR NATURAL HUMAN HABIT IS TO HOPE CONTIN-
ually for a life of nothing but happiness and pleasure.
We're always searching for a way not to feel any of the unpleasant stuff. But we can only embark wholeheartedly on a
genuine spiritual path when we start getting the haunting
sense that this dream will never come true. Unless we have
some inkling of this reality, it will be hard for us to move
toward opening to the wholeness of life. Instead we will
continue to follow the habits that keep us stuck in repetitive
anxiety and dissatisfaction, for generation after generation
across time.

The Buddha spoke a lot about the importance of working
with one's ego. But what did he mean by "ego"? There are various ways to talk about this word, but one definition I particularly like is "that which resists what is." Ego struggles against

reality, against the open-endedness and natural movement of life. It is very uncomfortable with vulnerability and ambiguity, with not being quite sure how to pin things down.

A few years ago, I was asked to give a graduation speech at Naropa University.* I thought a lot about what I could say to a group of people who were about to go into the world, where they had no idea what would happen. Of course, none of us know what is going to happen, but graduating from college can be an especially challenging transition. For a few years, you have your familiar campus, your student lifestyle and routines. Then, suddenly, things are no longer set in the same way, and your life becomes wide open.

I thought about how in education there's a lot of emphasis on success, but very little on failure. So, I decided to talk about the fine art of failure. As I told the students, learning how to fail will help us more than anything else in life—in the next six months, the next year, the next ten years, the next twenty years, for as long as we live, until we drop dead.

When we fail—in other words, when things don't work out the way we want them to—we feel our vulnerability in a raw and powerful way. Our uncomfortable ego tries to escape from that rawness. One of the most common methods is to blame our failure on something outside of us. Our relationship doesn't work out, so we blame the other person—or perhaps their entire gender. We can't get a job, so we blame our potential employers, or society as a whole, or the current political situation. The other common approach is to feel bad about ourselves and label ourselves a failure. Either way, we

---

* For the full text of this speech, see Pema Chödrön, *Fail, Fail Again, Fail Better* (Louisville, CO: Sounds True, 2015).

often end up feeling there's something fundamentally wrong with us.

There's a third way, however, which is to train ourselves simply to feel what we feel. I like to call this "holding the rawness of vulnerability in our heart." When we're resisting or trying to escape from "what is," there is usually some kind of physical sign—a tightening or contraction somewhere in the body. When you notice this sign of resistance, see if you can stick with the raw feeling of discomfort just for a moment, just long enough for your nervous system to start getting used to it.

Trungpa Rinpoche once said that we don't have the patience to stay with uncomfortable feelings for even three minutes. When I heard that, I thought, "Three minutes! That would be enough to win you some kind of grand prize!" For most of us these days, staying with discomfort for even three seconds is a lot of work! But whatever the amount of time, the idea is to keep increasing it gradually, at your own pace. Keep allowing yourself to hang in there for just a bit longer.

You may have a fixed idea of what you're experiencing, such as dread, anger, or disappointment. But when you let yourself be present with the feeling and experience it directly, you find that you can't pin it down so easily. That "dread" or "anger" keeps morphing and shifting and changing. Even though its unpleasantness haunts you, even though it feels so threatening, when you look hard you discover that you can't really find anything substantial.

The ego wants resolution, wants to control impermanence, wants something secure and certain to hold on to. It freezes what is actually fluid, it grasps at what is in motion, it tries to escape the beautiful truth of the fully alive nature of everything. As a result, we feel dissatisfied, haunted, threatened. We spend much of our time in a cage created by our own fear of discomfort.

The alternative to this struggle is to train in holding the rawness of vulnerability in our heart. Through this practice, we can eventually accustom our nervous systems to relaxing with the truth, to relaxing with the impermanent, uncontrollable nature of things. We can slowly increase our ability to expand rather than contract, to let go rather than cling.

Every time we practice holding the rawness of vulnerability in our heart, we gain a little insight into how things really are. We experience directly how nothing ever stays the same, even for a moment. We can't make anything stand still, even if we try. What we see, hear, smell, taste, touch, and think about is constantly changing. Even our heaviest, most unpleasant emotions have no solidity to them.

There's a music video of Beyoncé's song "Pretty Hurts" where she really captures what it's like to feel like a failure. Her feeling is so raw, and she just puts it all out there into the song. You realize that even though she's a roaring success and everything is going her way, she couldn't have made the video unless she had some real experience of what it feels like to fail. When we're able to hold the rawness of vulnerability in our hearts, we can use that energy to create poetry, writing, dance, music, song. We can make of it something that touches and communicates with other people. Artists have done this from the beginning of time.

If we close down to our unpleasant feelings without awareness or curiosity, if we always mask ourselves or try to make our vulnerability go away, out of that space come addictions of all kinds. Out of that space come aggression, striking out, violence against others—all the ugly things. On the other hand, if we can go beyond blame and other escapes and just feel the bleeding, raw meat quality of our vulnerability, we can enter a space where the best part of us comes out. Our bravery, our kindness, our ability to care about and reach out to others—all our best human qualities—come out of that space.

We all have tremendous potential and yet we stay closed in a very small, fearful world, based on wanting to avoid the unpleasant, the painful, the insecure, the unpredictable. There is vast, limitless richness and wonder we could experience if we fully accustomed our nervous systems to the open-ended, uncertain reality of how things are.

As Trungpa Rinpoche said, "There are sounds that you've never heard, smells that you've never smelled, sights that you've never seen, thoughts that you've never thought. The world is astoundingly full of potential for further and further and further opening, experiencing it wider and wider and wider." When we learn how to hold the rawness of vulnerability in our hearts, we will be able to experience our minds and hearts as vast as the universe.

5

The Path of Non-Rejecting

Only by learning to fully embrace all aspects of
ourselves—even the most seemingly negative elements
of our minds and hearts—will we learn to fully embrace
others. Only by discovering the basic goodness in both
our lotus and our mud, will we come to see the
basic goodness of all living beings.

I N THE BUDDHIST TEACHINGS, WE OFTEN COME ACROSS
the analogy of the lotus and the mud. A lotus has its roots
in mud. It rises through muddy water until it pierces the sur-
face and blossoms as a gorgeous flower that delights all who
see it. The lotus represents the beauty and purity of our fundamental nature—in other words, our basic goodness. And
what about that sticky, yucky mud? That symbolizes everything negative within us, everything that we would like to
move beyond: our confusion, our self-destructive habits, our
tendencies to hide out in a polarized mind and a closed heart.
By working through and rising above all these negativities,
we discover our basic goodness and achieve our full potential
as human beings.

But although this profound analogy has helped many people throughout the ages, it can easily be misinterpreted to contain an element of rejection. We may think the point is to reject the part of us that is mud in favor of the part that is lotus. We may hope to get rid of all the yucky and keep only what we consider beautiful. But this approach will only intensify our struggle with ourselves and add another layer to our emotional inner conflicts. And it will hinder our practice of bodhichitta because it will prevent us from connecting to the universal human predicament.

Over the years, my teachers have guided me toward a more refined way of approaching this topic. A phrase I like very much, which comes from Anam Thubten Rinpoche, is "the path of non-rejecting." As he wrote in a letter to his students a few years ago, the "wisdom teachings tell us not to reject anything about ourselves and embrace all aspects as the same. Gold is the same as dust. The lotus is part of the mud."

When we experience painful, unwelcome, difficult, or embarrassing feelings of any kind, we usually tend to escalate the emotion or to repress it. This often happens without our realizing what we're doing. When we become more conscious of what's going on in our mind, we may think we should now fight against our old habits and out-of-control emotions. We may react based on ideas of good and bad, worthy and unworthy. But the teachings encourage us to go beyond these limiting, polarizing, and often erroneous judgments and not turn against any part of ourselves. Instead, we can adopt an attitude that, from a conventional point of view, is quite radical: we can acknowledge all the things that we consider negative about ourselves and embrace them as we would our so-called positive qualities.

This may sound like a daring and exciting idea, but how do we actually put it into practice? How do we adopt this counterintuitive attitude when our emotions and neuroses hit us hard, in the painful, nontheoretical way that they do? I have learned a few effective methods, two of which I will share here.

The first method is based on a teaching by Tulku Thondup Rinpoche. When any unwanted feeling comes up, the first step is to feel it as fully as you can at the present moment. In other words, hold the rawness of vulnerability in your heart. Breathe with it, allow it to touch you, to inhabit you—open to it as fully as you currently can. Then make that feeling even stronger, even more intense. Do this in any way that works for you—in any way that makes the feeling stronger and more solid. Do this until the feeling becomes so heavy you could hold it in your hand. At that point, grab the feeling. And then just let it go. Let it float where it will, like a balloon, anywhere in the vast realm of empty space. Let it float out and out into the universe, dispersing into smaller and smaller particles, which become inconceivably tiny and distant.

This is not a practice of getting rid of the mud, but rather a way of putting our emotions, thoughts, problems, and issues—any of the "bad stuff" we normally don't want—into perspective. Instead of escalating, repressing, or rejecting, we intentionally contact the feeling, lean into it, intensify it, and then let it go into a new context—the vast, all-accommodating space of the universe. I have found this method to be especially helpful and accessible when I'm hooked, and my emotions feel very real and solid.

The second non-rejecting method is *tonglen*, which in Tibetan means "sending and taking." With this radical practice, we reverse our habitual tendencies to cling to pleasure and reject pain, to cling to comfort and reject discomfort—in other words, to grasp at what we want and push away what we don't want. These tendencies, which are based largely on fear and confusion, are what prevent us from fully awakening to our basically good nature. They are also the main hindrances to our ability to be there for others and help them also to awaken.

Here I'll give a general overview of the practice and its accompanying attitude. (You can find step-by-step instructions on the mechanics of tonglen practice in the practices section at the end of this book.) When we practice tonglen, we coordinate our mind with our breath. With every out-breath, we *send;* with every in-breath, we *take.* I'll begin with the taking aspect, which has a more obvious connection to the topic of non-rejection. During each inhalation, you imagine you're breathing in the unpleasant things you would normally reject. If you feel fear and don't want to experience this feeling—the edgy, speedy, nerve-racking, gnawing anxiety— instead of immediately jumping to get rid of it, you breathe it in. Instead of reacting against it, you welcome it and open to it. You breathe it into your heart, and as you continue to take it in during every in-breath, there's a sense of your heart expanding and expanding—becoming as wide as it needs to become in order to fully relax with those sensations. You could also bring it into your whole body, thinking of your body as wide-open space—a space that can accommodate any feelings, even intense ones.

As Trungpa Rinpoche once said, "It's as if you're the sky, allowing all the clouds to pass through you, not rejecting anything that arises in that space." I like this kind of imagery because it shows that tonglen is more of an art than an exact science. It's more like poetry or finger painting. You find your way by using your heart.

You start by breathing in something that you're personally feeling, but then you widen your scope to include all the people who are feeling the same thing. You aim to cultivate the brave attitude of being willing to take it on for everyone.

At times we may hesitate with this part of the practice because we're afraid of what we're breathing in. We may find ourselves taking only shallow breaths, as if we're worried about catching something. If we do tonglen for someone with an illness, we may fear that it could cause us to get the illness. But tonglen doesn't infect us with new forms of suffering that are not already within us. Rather, it heals our own pain by connecting us to the universal experience of being alive. Tonglen goes far beyond specific conditions. To the degree that we can open to our own discomfort, we can open to others' as well, and vice versa. This is so because in reality there's no difference between our pain and that of others. Fear is fear. Sadness is sadness. Anger is anger. Anxiety is anxiety. Whether we call them "mine" or "yours," they're more like free-floating qualities that we all share. When you breathe in "your" anxiety, you are opening to anxiety as a whole—the sum total of anxiety in this world. You can breathe it in, relax with it, make friends with it—and thus become free of it. And at the same time, you can make the wish that all other beings also be free of their own anxieties.

Sometimes the worse we feel, the more profound our tonglen practice is. The more acutely we experience painful emotions, the more clearly we understand what so many others are going through. This understanding deepens our compassion. It makes us want to remove others' pain just as much as we want to remove our own. It lends purpose to our lives. The more compassion we have for others, the more we can sense and enjoy our basic goodness. For this reason, adverse experiences—if we know how to meet them without rejection—are the most powerful means by which we can awaken. This is why I like to say that bad karma is our big chance.

The "sending" aspect of tonglen comes from another angle, but it also fosters this feeling of openness and connection to the experience of others. Each time we exhale, we imagine sending other beings all the beneficial and pleasurable things we normally desire for ourselves. Sometimes you can be very concrete. For instance, if you're thinking about a homeless person, you could breathe out food and shelter. Or you can send others universal qualities that everyone could use, such as kindness, well-being, relaxation, and warmth—this is how I tend to approach the practice. In the case of the homeless person, I might send them the feeling of being loved because I know how important it is for people to feel loved, especially when they are outcast by society.

The "sending" aspect of tonglen enriches our lives in two ways. It helps us increase our compassion and care for others. And it helps us let go of the tendency to hold on to what we like in an unrealistic and painful way. When it's a beautiful sunny day and the birds are singing, and everyone is smiling at us, we tend to cling to those nice feelings. We want this experience or situation to last as long as possible, and we feel a natural aversion to anything that threatens it. This self-protectiveness is a sign that beneath the joy there is an element of subtle fear.

We can make better use of our good fortune—and enjoy it even more wholeheartedly—by incorporating it into tonglen. Good health, delicious food, beautiful weather, warm family time, a sense of accomplishment or recognition, a feeling of inner peace—when any of the pleasant experiences that everyone desires come our way, we can mentally share them with others. We can wish that they enjoy these pleasures just as much as we do, or even more.

The two aspects of sending and taking reinforce and support each other, so it's most effective to do them alternately, riding on each breath. When we inhale and open ourselves up to our own unwanted feelings and those of others—when we welcome the unwelcome—we discover greater spaciousness in our hearts and minds. We feel relieved to be no longer fighting off each unpleasant experience that arises. When we exhale, we can send this spaciousness and relief to others who are similarly struggling against their feelings. Whatever inner freedom and contentment we've gained through our practice of non-rejection we can offer to all other people and living beings that need these qualities just as much as we do. We can radiate our basic goodness from our whole body, sending it out to more and more beings—across countries, continents, and worlds—until it pervades all space.

These practices of non-rejection are powerful means of nurturing our bodhichitta and overcoming polarization. Only by learning to fully embrace all aspects of ourselves—even the most seemingly negative elements of our minds and hearts—will we learn to fully embrace others. Only by discovering the basic goodness in both our lotus and our mud, will we come to see the basic goodness of all living beings.

6

Just as It Is

The wonderful irony about this spiritual journey is that we find it only leads us to become just as we are. The exalted state of enlightenment is nothing more than fully knowing ourselves and our world, just as we are.

WE ALL HAVE MOMENTS OF APPRECIATING WHAT we see or taste or smell—just as it is. We relax and out of nowhere we accept our experience without wanting anything to be more or less or different. We feel that everything, at least for the moment, is complete.

When our mind is open and fresh, we see beauty everywhere, including within ourselves. There's a sense of savoring the uniqueness of each moment. Things have never been just the way they are now. Nor will they ever be just this way again. We're in tune with the transience of the world, with its poignancy and its profound richness.

The idea of appreciating things just as they are is simple and accessible, but it's also very profound. It's the key to feeling warm and loving toward others and toward ourselves. This ability to open, to experience things freshly, is always present in our mind. We may not sense it at all times, but it is waiting in the background. The question then is how to uncover this ability, how to contact it, how to nurture it. How can we learn to spend more and more of our time in this state of mind? How can we develop trust in the completeness of "just as it is"?

The first step is to realize the importance of how we choose to orient our minds. We may find that we're habitually focused on incompleteness. We have thoughts such as "I am unworthy, I am lacking, the world is nothing but problems." With this outlook, we will see imperfection wherever we look and always feel dissatisfied.

To begin healing this negative orientation, one simple approach is to practice noting whatever we appreciate. We can take note of even the most ordinary things, such as the way the light hits someone's face or reflects off the side of a building. It could be the taste of your ordinary lunch, with its various shades of sweet, salty, sour, or bitter. It could be a piece of music or a painting or the way someone moves. It could be a voice you hear. Maybe a stranger has just opened her mouth and you discover to your surprise that she has a beautiful accent. To appreciate people and things in this way doesn't take a big effort, but it warms our hearts and makes us feel connected to the world. It's a lot more pleasant than collecting grievances from morning till night, which can easily happen if we just let ourselves go with the momentum of our habits.

We can also make a point of appreciating all that we have. In my case, now that I'm in my eighties, I could be complaining about my physical pain, my wrinkles, my dental problems—all kinds of things come to mind. And sometimes

I do complain! But if my practice is appreciation, I can think about how I'm still able to go for long walks. My older sister, who used to be a big hiker, has arthritic feet and can no longer walk far. She has a good spirit, so she doesn't complain. But her arthritis makes me realize, every time I go for a walk, how grateful I am for my legs and feet and hips. How wonderful that they all work, and I can be refreshed and invigorated by my walks, rather than end up in so much pain that I don't want to do it anymore.

We can lose these abilities at any time. But I still have my eyesight and, even though it's not what it used to be, and I need reading glasses, I can still experience all the colors of the rainbow. I can see the changing of the seasons, the wetness on leaves, the wind blowing the trees. And my hearing is still pretty good. One of my friends has lost most of his hearing, to the point where hearing aids don't really help. One day, he put his hand on mine and said, "I would give anything to just be able to sit and listen to the birds." And I thought, I *can* listen to the birds. I really need to bring that ability into focus and appreciate it while I have it.

Another practice in this area, which I used to experiment with frequently, is to pay special attention to strangers you encounter in daily life. One of the first times I tried this was with a bank teller. While she did her calculations, I made a point of seeing her as a living human being. Miraculously, this anonymous teller, whose only function, seemingly, was to count my money, started to become a woman who had a life, a job, friends, activities, likes and dislikes. I noticed her clothing, her hair, the way she moved her hands. I imagined what she did before coming to work that day: how she chose her outfit, applied her makeup, and—just before leaving the house—made the spontaneous decision to put on the earrings her friend had recently given her. This exercise brought about a feeling of uncontrived care for this anonymous woman. I felt warm toward her simply because she was a human being with a life.

When we make an effort to notice people and use our imagination in this way, we begin to feel our sameness with everyone. All of us are the center of our own universe, and at the same time, we are anonymous people that others don't even see. We all have full lives with our own versions of joy and sorrow, hope and fear. If we take the time to appreciate others in this way, the strangers we encounter become mirrors showing us our own humanity and vulnerability. Then we can turn the natural warmth that arises toward others into a natural warmth toward ourselves.

We can feel this warmth not only toward the things we find easy to like about ourselves, but also toward what tends to upset or displease us. Our bad habits, our fears, our haunting thought that something is fundamentally wrong with us—whatever temporary or chronic neurosis we are going through—these are just a part of who we are, at least for the moment. We can allow space for these uncomfortable thoughts and emotions to be there, not rejecting them but also not buying into them. With this attitude of nonjudgment, we can develop genuine appreciation toward ourselves, just as we are. This will help us get to know and trust our basic goodness, which is complete, with nothing lacking.

Talking about appreciating the world "just as it is" and ourselves "just as we are" is another way of talking about the path of non-rejection. As we walk on this path, we can apply active practices such as sending and taking. But other times we can experiment with a simpler approach. We can try just sitting with it all—our thoughts, our feelings, our perceptions—and letting everything be just as it is.

In his teaching on the lotus and the mud, Anam Thubten says, "All flaws that exist are part of us. They begin to heal on their own when we accept them as they are. They can be fertilizer for our inner growth. Recognizing them without denying or maneuvering around them is the key point." In some ways this practice of accepting and letting be is an even more radical approach than tonglen. Could it really be true that our neurotic habits and dysfunctional patterns will begin to heal on their own if we just stay present with them instead of indulging or running away? This is something worth contemplating deeply and trying out as best as we currently can.

Anam Thubten emphasizes that this brave acknowledgment of our "flaws" is not about indulging in feelings of shame or guilt. It is, instead, about "not hiding anything from one's awareness." Instead of reacting in one way or another, we can simply choose not to hide anything from our own mind. We can regard all that we observe simply as karmic seeds ripening. Whatever arises in our mind and heart is just our current experience, nothing more or less. Even our good and bad qualities are temporary and insubstantial, not ultimate proofs of our worthiness or unworthiness. They are not inherent to our fundamental nature of basic goodness; they are simply what is. If we learn to work with our experiences in this way, then instead of succumbing to the pull of our old habits, we can stay present with them until they calm down of their own accord.

When you feel yourself closing down, hardening, and tightening against this precious world or your dear old self, you can use "just as it is" as an antidote. It's a mantra that you can apply on the spot, whenever needed. Simply saying, "This experience is complete just as it is," or "I am complete just as I am," is a way of catching yourself as you begin to divide your experience in half—into this against that or me against you. It's a way of catching yourself just as you begin to harden into a dualistic way of perceiving, a view that inevitably brings struggle and dissatisfaction.

Trungpa Rinpoche referred to basic goodness as "unstoppable brilliance." This means that sooner or later—no matter how stubborn or lazy or dubious we are—confidence in our basic goodness and the basic goodness of the world will dawn on us. We will develop complete trust in our experience "just as it is." It's inevitable.

The wonderful irony about this spiritual journey is that we find it only leads us to become just as we are. The exalted state of enlightenment is nothing more than fully knowing ourselves and our world, just as we are. In other words, the ultimate fruition of this path is simply to be fully human. And the ultimate benefit we can bring to others is to help them also realize their full humanity, just as they are.

7

How Not to Lose Heart

*As we individuals grow in our resilience—as we become
better at staying conscious and not losing heart—we will
be able to remain strong in challenging conditions for the
long haul. This is within the capacity of all of us.*

I MET A MAN WHO'S BEEN WORKING FOR MANY YEARS
with gang violence in Los Angeles, predominantly in
Latino neighborhoods. He's always having to pursue funding
for his work, and in the proposals he writes, he needs to be
very positive: everything is going forward, change is happening, it's all great. But even though he's been successful in
helping people get jobs and find a positive direction for their
lives, when he writes those proposals, he feels like a hypo-
crite. He feels that things may look good on paper, but in
reality, the whole situation isn't getting better. Almost every
day, he hears about some tragedy. A man has gotten his life
together, he has a good job and a family, and then one day he's
out washing his car and he gets shot and killed. And all that
good work is gone.

Many of us who are engaged with the world experience

discouragement regularly. If you're concerned about the environment, social justice and equity, prison reform, the welfare of immigrants, or the welfare of people and the planet in general, it's very easy to lose heart.

But even though there are many situations that seem unfixable, I feel it's important not to lose heart. The question then becomes: How? How do we not let ourselves spiral downward into a mindset of increasing hopelessness and negativity? Or, if we're already finding ourselves going downhill, how do we pull ourselves up?

One encouraging thing I hear over and over, from people working in all kinds of fields, is that they see a lot of basic goodness in people. My friend Jarvis Masters has been on death row in California since 1985. Most of his friends and neighbors have murdered people. But he said to me once, "I've never met anybody where I didn't see their basic goodness. When you really talk to these guys, there's so much regret and heartbreak and sad family history. You begin to see their tenderness, their basic goodness."

The reason we often start to go downhill with losing heart is that we allow ourselves to get hooked by our emotions. We may get justifiably enraged against the government or the corporations or the boss—whoever seems to be obstructing justice. But whatever the circumstances, once we get worked up in a major way, we lose our effectiveness. We lose our skill to communicate in such a way that change is really possible. We lose our ability to do the one thing that is most often within our reach—to uplift ourselves and the people we encounter.

When we get hooked—when we get really angry, resentful, fearful, or selfish—we start to go a little unconscious. We lose our *payu*—our awareness of what we're doing with our body, speech, and mind. In this state, it's all too easy to let ourselves spiral downward. The first step in pulling yourself up is to notice and acknowledge when you're going unconscious. Without doing that, nothing can get better for you. How could you change anything if you're not aware of what's going on?

It may sound tricky to be conscious of the fact that you're unconscious. But if you pay attention to when you're getting worked up, you'll be able to read the signs. When you get hooked, you lose your sense of everyone having the same vulnerability, of everyone holding the same desire to have happiness and to avoid pain. You find yourself cut off from the human condition, in a state where things don't touch you.

Imagine you are in a beautiful place, with plenty of comfort, luxury, good food, and pleasant companions. It sounds like where most of us would want to be all the time, but if you're in this atmosphere it becomes hard to relate to any sort of suffering in the world. You may hear news that people just got blown up somewhere in the Middle East, but it doesn't really get through.

Then there's the situation of being cut off because of loss of heart. Here you lose your ability to discern the basic goodness in people. You lose your ability to discern what can and can't be fixed. You lose your confidence in general. And from here, it's easy to go into a downward cycle of discouragement—a self-fulfilling view of yourself and humanity as unworthy.

Whether or not we let ourselves go unconscious has huge implications, not just for ourselves, but for all of society. Trungpa Rinpoche said that if enough people have confidence in basic goodness and our ability to pull ourselves up and be there for others, then when the challenges become great, instead of going down, society will grow stronger.

After the planes flew into the World Trade Center, many New Yorkers pulled together. Everyone's sense of reality was so blown apart that nothing made sense except to help each other. That was true for a little while, but then the trauma of the whole event kicked in and people started to close down in fear. They started to lose consciousness. A few months after the event, a *New Yorker* cartoon showed one woman saying to another: "It's hard, but slowly I'm getting back to hating everyone." This pattern is what we observe in many difficult situations. For instance, if someone is very ill, everyone pulls together to help, but if the illness goes on for a year or two, people start pulling away because they're not up for that much.

As we individuals grow in our resilience—as we become better at staying conscious and not losing heart—we will be able to remain strong in challenging conditions for the long haul. This is within the capacity of all of us. From my own experience I know this to be true. I used to let myself go into a downward spiral, but having practiced meditation and received teachings for many years, when things start to get bad, I perk up. When I become aware that I'm closing down, I actually get a little excited. Here is a chance to reverse the old pattern and pull myself up! It's taken me about eighty years to get to this point, but I know that if I can do it, everyone can. We all start at different levels of unconsciousness, but wherever we are, we can always improve with practice.

When we are losing heart because of our own struggles in life, one of the best antidotes is to put things in a bigger context. Sometimes this just happens naturally. For example,

I was working with a student who's a wonderful person, but completely stuck in certain areas of his life. He had a habit of turning inward on himself that resulted in him feeling like a victim. He was always saying, "Why me?" I tried to give him good advice; for years, he went to therapy and did many brave things to work with his issues; but nothing worked. Despite his obvious basic goodness and strength, nothing was getting through to him.

Then he found out he had incurable cancer. Overnight, his habitual pattern was remedied. Soon after, I was in a car with him and someone was walking slowly through the crosswalk after the light had changed. He started to get angry, which was his habit in those situations, but then he abruptly stopped and said, "I don't have time to get pissed off at someone for walking across the street too slowly."

He also had some very stuck relationships, particularly with his mother. They couldn't stop doing the same dance. But after his cancer diagnosis, he was on the phone with her and when she said something that would normally trigger him, he said, "Mom, I'm probably going to die soon, and I don't have time to do this to you anymore." It all changed overnight. His years of meditation and therapy had helped set the stage, but it was only when he put things in a bigger context that he could actually break free from his habits.

Finding out we don't have much time left can help enlarge our perspective, but not everyone suddenly gets a bad cancer report. We don't have to depend on a dramatic or life-threatening event to wake us up. Again, I think of my friend Jarvis, who sees things from a big perspective because he's spent so much time developing his compassion. Once he was in the prison yard and a guard started taunting him, trying to goad him into reacting. But Jarvis didn't take the bait. Then his friends said, "How can you take that from him? How can you be so calm? Is it your Buddhism that does that?" And he said, "No, it's not my Buddhism. I've gotten letters from the kids of guards, who tell me that when their parent has a hard day they come home and take it out on their family. I didn't want this man to go home and beat his kids." So, compassion can enlarge our view as well. You think about the wider consequences of getting hooked and you don't let yourself act in a way that brings pain to other people.

As someone once pointed out to me, when you become conscious, the first thing you discover is why you stayed unconscious all those years. Being conscious means you really have to feel what you feel, which is frequently very vulnerable and raw. My friend with cancer was willing to go to that vulnerable place because he didn't want to waste time on pettiness, when everything seemed trivial in the face of what was coming. Jarvis let himself be vulnerable to someone who had power over him because he knew what the consequences might be for the guard's family. By putting things in a bigger context, they were able to enter a whole realm of practice—learning to stay with the rawness of vulnerability of being human.

Widening our perspective and becoming more conscious individually also has a positive effect on our society. If enough of us can really feel what we feel, if enough of us can stay upright with our vulnerability instead of spiraling down, then that will naturally lead to more people being there for each other.

When I read the news or listen to people working in fields where things can get very disheartening, I get a certain feeling, which is a signal that I might start to go downhill. Everyone has their own thing that brings them down. For some, it's seeing how much aggression and violence there is in the world. For some it's rampant greed, or injustice, or insensitivity to others' pain. What really gets me, as I've already mentioned, is seeing the polarization that's so prevalent right now: polarization based on religion, race, sexual preference, social class—all the ways in which our minds and hearts get tight about our positions, all the ways in which we close down into "us" and "them." Since polarization is the most potentially disheartening thing for me, I'll use how I've been working with it as an example.

The first step is to look for polarization in myself. This involves arousing enough bravery to feel the vulnerability of seeing my own neurosis—to sit up straight with it instead of collapsing and hiding. When I honestly look for polarization in myself, I find a lot of digging in my heels and seeing the other as the problem. I find a lot of seeing other human beings as adversaries, with nothing but faults—in contrast to my own faultlessness. People have always been quick to remind me that I have these habits, but I can't really see them without taking a closer look.

Once I bring my own habits into focus, I make a strong aspiration to do everything possible not to add any more polarization to the world. This is a way of placing my actions in a bigger context. I'm no longer just doing my shtick, reacting in my habitual knee-jerk way to whatever bothers me. Once I make this aspiration, it becomes easier for me to apply an antidote to whatever uncomfortable feeling is pushing me in the direction of polarizing. For example, I can practice tonglen or simply let the feeling be there, just as it is.

So far, I can't claim this to be a great success story. It's a work in progress. But now I'm often able to have a wider view of my own polarization. This isn't about being a good girl and sitting up nicely and not badmouthing people anymore. It's not about "Nice people don't do that—especially nuns." The point is not to shame or scold myself or put myself in the category of "bad people." But if I think about the larger societal repercussions, it's easier to stop doing it. Like many tiny drops filling a bucket with water, it takes a lot of people like me holding a grudge against others to create a polarized society. I really don't want to be one of those drops.

Here's another example. A woman I know was really heartbroken when she thought about how many people in the world feel like there's something wrong with them. When you have millions or billions of people denigrating themselves, you have millions or billions of people going unconscious because they don't want to feel what they're feeling. It's easy to see that the result of this is not pretty. It's easy to see how it could be a large factor in why there's so much strife in our world. This woman began to look at her strong tendency to criticize herself in this bigger context. She didn't want to add more drops to the bucket of self-denigration. When she'd start feeling bad about herself or feeling like damaged goods, she'd just say, "I'm not going to do this because I don't want to add any more self-criticism to the planet."

The overall point here is that the way not to lose heart is to realize how everything we do matters. It can go either way. If we go toward defensiveness, closing down, and unconsciousness, we add those elements to a planet that already suffers enough from such tendencies. On the other hand, if we allow ourselves to feel our vulnerability, if we sit up tall when we want to collapse and refrain from striking out when we're provoked, we are having a positive effect on the larger world. Maintaining our own confidence and well-being benefits our family and our workplace and everyone we communicate with. Happiness is contagious.

When more of us learn to trust our basic goodness, society will get stronger. This doesn't mean there won't be hard times. It doesn't mean violence, injustice, and poverty will end. It doesn't mean the polar icecaps won't melt and the water in the oceans won't rise. But it does mean that there will be a lot of resilient people who will never give up on humanity and will always be around to help others. It does mean that when things get rough, it will bring out the best in people, rather than the worst. If we learn how not to lose heart, we will always find ways to make important contributions to our world.

8

Beyond the Comfort Zone

*The more willing you are to step out of your comfort zone,
the more comfortable you feel in your life. Situations that
used to arouse fear and nausea become easier to relax in.
On the other hand, if you stay in the comfort zone all the
time, it shrinks.*

A FEW YEARS AGO, I WROTE A LETTER TO MY STU-
dents in which I asked them about where they take
refuge: "When things are really tough—like you're scared,
you're lonely, you're angry, everything's falling apart, difficult
times—in what do you take refuge?" Usually I don't get answers to these letters, but this one got a lot of people writing. They found it to be such a helpful question because they
had to admit—which didn't surprise me at all—that in hard
times they were taking refuge in Netflix, or in overeating, or
in other types of entertainment and distraction.

Buddhist practitioners traditionally speak of taking refuge
in the Three Jewels. The Buddha is our example, role model,
and inspiration. The Dharma is the teachings of the Buddha
and other awakened beings like him. The Sangha is the

community of people who are also on the path of awakening. But when I asked my students where they really were going for refuge, many of them were honest enough to admit they weren't looking first to the Three Jewels. Instead, they were going for what was habitual and easy.

Trungpa Rinpoche used to describe most types of refuge as "comfort neurosis." When babies need comfort, they may suck their thumb. When things get difficult for adults, we generally do our own version of thumb-sucking. So, the question to ask yourself is, "What's my thumb?"

I came across a book called *True Refuge* by Tarchin Hearn, a teacher in New Zealand. He talks about how people at his dharma center say a chant every morning in which they take refuge in the Buddha, Dharma, and Sangha. But then he asks them to think further about what they really take refuge in when times are tough. Suppose it's streaming TV shows. His advice is to call it what it is. When you're just about to press "play," put your hands together and say, "I take refuge in Netflix." Or if food is your thing, when you're just about to open the refrigerator, put your hands together and say, "I take refuge in the refrigerator," or "I take refuge in this peanut butter sandwich I'm going to eat at two a.m."

To go deeper into this topic, I've found it helpful to use a model describing the process of growth invented by the Soviet psychologist Lev Vygotsky in the 1930s and developed more recently by PassageWorks, an educational group in Boulder, Colorado, where I first heard the phrase "Welcoming the unwelcome." This model can be illustrated with a diagram showing three concentric circles. The innermost circle is the "comfort zone." Around that is the "learning" or "challenge zone." The outermost circle is called the "excessive risk zone."

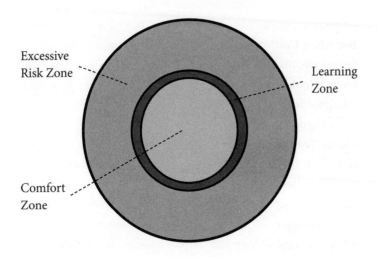

The comfort zone is what we're most attracted to. It's where we prefer to hang out. Now, I'm not saying there's anything inherently wrong with streaming movies. I'm a big movie lover myself. And everybody needs comfort. But if you spend the rest of your life only trying to be comfortable, watching Netflix every night with your peanut butter sandwich, that can be problematic. There are definitely more harmful ways to get comfortable, but we should ask ourselves: If we always stay in that narrow zone, how are we going to grow?

The learning zone is where we stretch beyond our comfort. Say you have a problem with stinginess. It runs deep within you. Giving things away feels like giving away your ground; it threatens your whole being. You can step into your learning zone by deciding to give away something very small. For instance, I often have a lot of trouble finding a pen that works well for me. When I finally find a good one, the thought of giving it away can even make me feel slightly nauseated. It may trigger deep attachment and security issues. But if I do give it away, I step into my learning zone. I feel the discomfort and see that I have survived. Then the next day, I can give away something else small—a postage stamp, a smile when I don't feel like smiling, anything that pushes the edge a little bit. The learning zone is provocative, but it's where most of our growth happens.

The outermost circle in this model is called the "excessive risk" zone. This area is usually too challenging to nurture growth. It's like being in the deep end of the swimming pool when you don't even know how to swim. You're just not ready to go there. If you force yourself to be in this outer zone, you'll be too traumatized to learn anything. Some people who push too hard in their dharma practice run away screaming and never meditate again. This kind of backlash can occur if you try to leap from your comfort to the outermost zone. But if you spend as much time as you can hanging out in your learning zone, eventually you'll be ready for some of these greater challenges.

Everyone's three zones are very personal to them. One person's excessive risk zone can be another person's learning zone. For example, I often think about the incredible courage of the Freedom Riders, who rode buses in the early sixties to challenge the segregation laws in the South. They went into situations where a lot of people were happy to insult them— or even kill them—experiences that for most people would be overwhelming. But not everyone was afraid. A few years ago, I met one of the Freedom Riders and I got the impression that for him, riding those buses was actually in his comfort zone. He thrived in that situation, so even risking his life felt comfortable. Maybe for him, having to stay in the office and take phone calls would have felt more challenging.

The interesting thing is that the more willing you are to step out of your comfort zone, the more comfortable you feel in your life. Situations that used to arouse fear and nausea become easier to relax in. On the other hand, if you stay in the comfort zone all the time, it shrinks. It can be that way in a gated community. The gate makes you feel protected. But what happens when your washing machine breaks down and someone has to come in and fix it? The more you try to wall off the danger, the more afraid you become of everyone. And the older you get, the more threatened you feel. Things that didn't bother you when you were thirty or forty can make you very uncomfortable when you're seventy or eighty.

In the context of refuge, I think it's very helpful to keep these three zones in mind and to notice our orientation. Sometimes we just have to say, "I need to be in my comfort zone right now because I'm stressed out and it would help me." If that's the case, honor that. But other times, we may discover that we're kidding ourselves. We can't honestly claim that we're taking refuge in the Three Jewels. We can't honestly say that we're following our intention to use our life to grow. But if we understand how growth happens and are inspired to pursue the path of awakening, we develop an appetite for the things that challenge us. We become increasingly drawn to the places where learning and deepening can happen.

In the fourteenth century, the Tibetan sage Thogme Zangpo wrote *The Thirty-Seven Practices of a Bodhisattva*, which is still one of the most quoted and beloved poems in Buddhist literature. Each of its stanzas gives advice on how to live like a bodhisattva, a person whose highest aspiration in life is to wake up for the benefit of all living beings. In one verse, he poignantly describes why a comfort-oriented lifestyle is unsatisfactory. Happiness "disappears in a moment," he says, "like a dewdrop on a blade of grass."* Basing your comfort on things that don't last is a futile strategy for living. Even when you get something you've always wanted, the pleasure you get lasts for such a short time.

The most poignant example is falling in love. That beginning glow part—the honeymoon stage—can last a couple of years. Then you have two people living together, which is when you really start dwelling in the learning zone. This is why relationships can be so powerful for our spiritual growth. If the relationship is to continue, stretching will be inevitable. That's when you start to deepen.

The idea of happiness disappearing like a dewdrop could sound depressing, but Thogme Zangpo's intention here is to point us to freedom. Clinging to things that are always changing is a comfort zone tactic. It's what keeps us in *samsara*, which is a Sanskrit word referring to the vicious cycle we're all trapped in because we continually resist reality. The only way to free ourselves from samsara is to awaken to the open-endedness of how things are. This requires venturing out into the learning zone, where we will encounter fundamental groundlessness. Trungpa Rinpoche equates this state with the wide-open space of our basic goodness. It is the fresh air of our deepest sanity. But because this space doesn't give us much to hang on to, we usually find it intimidating. This is when, in Trungpa Rinpoche's poetic description, we tend to "hide ourselves in caves and jungles," which is

---

* All quotations of Thogme Zangpo are translations by Ken McLeod that appear in *Reflections on Silver River* (Sonoma, CA: Unfettered Mind Media, 2014).

a way of saying we become very self-involved. We "kindle a great fire of hatred," "roil the river of lust," and "wallow in the mud of laziness." Aggression, passion, and ignorance—what are known as the three poisons—are the result of not connecting with our basic goodness because we fear the groundless state.

Tonglen is one of the most effective practices for changing our attitudes about comfort. Instead of following our habit of avoiding discomfort, we breathe in what we tend to find unpleasant or threatening. But again, we don't do this to the extent that we enter the excessive risk zone. Instead of jumping into our worst nightmares, we can work with unpleasantness at a lower intensity. We can use something small, such as disappointment—something unpleasant that would normally provoke a reaction, but not something overwhelming. You were planning on making a special meal, but you realize you're missing one of the main ingredients and it's too late to get it. You planned a picnic, but then it started raining. Or you were going to stream your favorite program, but your internet connection is down. Just by choosing to do tonglen in these situations, instead of losing heart or acting out, you're stepping out of your comfort zone. You're beginning to make friends with your own pain and to develop empathy with the human condition. Even though you're working with a relatively minor suffering, you're building the strength and capacity to handle something greater. If you keep doing this, you'll find that in great adversity, that strength will be available to you.

Then it's important to balance the in-breath with the out-breath. Matthieu Ricard, the well-known Buddhist monk and author, was once being tested for compassion by being hooked up to one of those big machines that records all your brain activity. He began by visualizing himself sending rays of healing light to those who are suffering, but the scientists wanted him instead to focus on breathing the suffering in. For that period, he saturated himself. He had just visited an orphanage in Romania where it was so sad to see how the children were being treated. And he'd also recently been in Tibet after an earthquake. So he had a lot of material, which he kept breathing in and breathing in.

From this experience, he said he learned that a person can only take so much. He found that taking on suffering had to be balanced with love and kindness, with the completeness of life. I think that this example illustrates how he approached the excessive risk zone, and realized that if you breathe in the pain, you also have to send out the love. There's a sense of connecting with both beauty and tragedy—with the delight-fulness and upliftedness of life, and with the degraded and cruel part of life.

In this very brief time that we have on earth, we have to ask ourselves how we're going to spend our time. Will we keep increasing and strengthening our neurotic habits in our vain quest for some kind of lasting comfort and pleasure? Or will we make it a practice to step out into the learning zone? It's almost terrifying how fast life goes by, especially at my age. Even though I move slowly and like a lot of space, there's this feeling that I'm rushing to catch up. At the end of each day, what did I do? Did I spend the day strengthening my com-fort orientation? Did I indulge in "nostalgia for samsara," as Trungpa Rinpoche liked to say, by longing for the time when I thought I just needed a lovely cup of tea to be happy? Or did I step out into groundlessness and truly take refuge in the

Three Jewels? Did I lighten up and loosen up, or did I hunker down in my armor and try to maintain the status quo?

Status quo is not very helpful for spiritual growth, for using this short interval between birth and death. On the other hand, expanding our ability to feel comfortable in our own skin and in the world, so that we can be there as much as possible for other people, is a very worthy way to spend a human life.

9

Speaking from Our Shared Humanity

*Bodhisattva speech communicates respect for yourself
and others, rather than disrespect, aggression, and
polarization. It is speech that comes from the
heart and communicates to the heart.*

I HAVE A CLOSE FRIEND WHO'S BEEN IN PRISON FOR about forty years, ever since he was a teenager. During this time, he's developed a lot of wisdom and insight about helping young people at risk. Recently, he was telling me how someone who lived among gangs could stay out of trouble. For instance, a young man wants to avoid going over to a friend's house because he knows he's likely to get drawn into a violent situation. What should he do? I wondered: Wouldn't it just make everyone angry if he didn't go? Wouldn't that make his friends judge him, and wouldn't that result in further polarization?

My friend said, "It all depends how you talk to them. If you said, 'No way! You guys are nothing but trouble!' then, yes, that would be a problem. But if you said, 'I'm not coming over because my mother is drunk and I have to take care of her,' everyone would understand. Or if you said, 'I need to study for a test and my teacher says if I do well, I could succeed in this world,' everyone would support you."

Deep down, everyone supports people doing well in their lives. We all have basic goodness, which naturally responds to the basic goodness of others. But the right conditions have to be there for this positive inclination to come out. How we communicate is crucial. When we set ourselves apart and speak from our neurosis to others' neurosis, we create further division. But when we come from a place of shared humanity, our speech can have the effect of healing.

For me, this is the meaning of bodhisattva speech. It communicates respect for yourself and others, rather than disrespect, aggression, and polarization. It is speech that comes from the heart and communicates to the heart.

Trungpa Rinpoche talked about creating situations that encourage people to connect with their own basic goodness. We can learn to speak in a way that brings ourselves and others closer to the sanity of our own basic nature. This is one of the most important skills for the bodhisattva to develop.

Many years ago, I shared a house with a good friend. We got along well, but then something uncomfortable began to happen in our relationship. Every day we would talk about other people. And we were only interested in people we could criticize. We would say nasty things ("He does that" and "Did you see what she did?") while pretending that we were trying to be understanding and helpful. It was poisonous. Sometimes I would wake up in the morning and make a resolution: "Today, I'm just going to listen but not get involved with criticizing." But it was impossible. Isn't it just too delicious when someone sees things the way you do and criticizes the very person you feel critical about? This went on for a long time. Then, one day, without planning, I found myself saying to her, "Let's not do this anymore." And sure enough, she had also been trying to extricate herself from our unwholesome dance. So we were able to drop it right then.

In a sense I got lucky that my friend wasn't offended when I blurted out my thought. Until I spoke, I didn't know we were on the same page. But I think it worked because I wasn't coming from a place of knowing better than my friend, and she understood that.

Speaking from the heart brings us closer together. It comes from seeing that our true state is interconnected. Our speech uncovers that interconnectedness instead of reinforcing the misunderstanding that we're separate. On the other hand, if we look down on someone, seeing him or her as inherently problematic or threatening, our speech will reflect the polarization in our mind.

Sometimes we have the best intentions to bring about positive change, but we're too caught up in our ego-clinging to carry them out. We're too triggered to have good judgment. In these cases, our speech and actions are more likely to divide than unite. The classic ridiculous example is the antiwar protestors who end up using their peace signs to clobber the people who disagree with them. Our natural intelligence knows what will make matters better and what will make them worse—what will cool off a situation and what will inflame it. But when we're coming from a place of anger or irritation or feeling threatened, our intelligence is muddied. When we feel worked up, we lose our perspective. Our attitude becomes, "I'm so together, so sane, so reasonable. Unlike *those* people." Not surprisingly, this tends to be the time when we have the greatest desire to speak.

We all have some peculiar things that get to us. For instance, you may not be able to stand hearing people make loud, smacking noises when they eat. You may feel that the only way to express your genuine self is to say, "That sound is disgusting!" That's not speaking from the heart. When we speak from emotional reactivity, there's no sense of shared humanity.

This isn't to say we should avoid addressing outer circumstances. Parents, for example, need to guide the behavior of their children. And there are far too many injustices in the world. But if we're to speak in a way that actually helps, we first need to work with our own propensities when they are triggered. Then, if we want to become activists, we can be more effective because we'll enter situations with a clear head—not blinded by anger or other emotions. If you have no intense feelings about lip smacking but think that it's in everyone's best interest for the person to stop, you can say something, and your words are more likely to be well received.

The Dharma always brings us back to ourselves. Before we can heal others with our speech, we need to get a handle on our own mind and its propensities. This is why bodhisattvas long to attain enlightenment—to wake up fully so that they can be of greatest benefit to others. We all want our communication to be helpful, but when we sit and look within, we may notice that we're the mirror image of the people we want to help. We begin to say, "My goodness! How alike we all are! Maybe those other people aren't that much more neurotic than I am!"

Here is an example of wise and honest self-reflection. A young Jewish woman I know spent a summer in Israel. She found herself in an environment with a lot of conflict, especially about political views. Many people she met were completely convinced about how right they were. She wanted to have a positive influence but was afraid that if she spoke, she would do more harm than good. Ironically, her work focused on empowering people to find their voice, but in this situation, she was unable to find her own. Then she looked into her mind and found where she was stuck: she was being too judgmental of others. She could easily see the rigidity in others' hearts, but she realized that until she could soften her own heart, her speech would be ineffective.

Coming to terms with what we find in ourselves can be painful. But if we can learn to sit with the raw pain of that self-discovery—if we can sit with and bear that uncomfortable feeling—that itself will soften our heart. It will make us more humble. Because all of us are really quite vulnerable, when we speak to others unskillfully—from our reactivity— it's all too easy to open up wounds. But when we speak from our own vulnerable good heart, what comes out of our mouth is more likely to be healing than divisive. Instead of making others feel bad about themselves, our speech can help them connect to what is best within themselves.

Skillful communication is based on discernment. We need discernment to know when it's time to speak and when it's not—when it's time to say firmly, "Stop it, that's hurtful" or to speak softly and gently. Most of all, we need discernment about ourselves. What triggers or hooks us? How do we reach the point where our discomfort spills out into actions we regret? What calms our agitated mind, instead of pouring kerosene on the fire?

I often quote Shantideva, a great Buddhist sage from the eighth century whose writings are widely taught to this day. His advice to keep ourselves from escalating is to "remain like a log of wood." He lists many provocative situations and then recommends that we don't act or speak when they come up. Often people interpret this advice as repression. But the point is that remaining like a log interrupts the momentum of our habitual reactions, which usually make things worse. Instead of reacting, we rest with the moving, heightened energy that has arisen. We let ourselves just experience what we're experiencing. This slows down the process and allows some space to open up. It gives us a chance to discern our inner process and then do something different. And when we're interacting with another person, it also allows them a chance to cool down and connect with their basic goodness.

But speaking from the heart doesn't just come to us automatically. It's not usually second nature. It's actually a skill that we need to work on. We need to keep refining our capacity to speak skillfully, year after year, for our entire lives. This process requires trial and error. We have to make many mistakes and be willing to learn from them. Dzigar Kongtrul Rinpoche once told me that to grow in wisdom I had to "learn the hard way." I took that to mean I would only learn how to be more skillful by *not* getting it right.

Even if we first look within and make sure that we're seeing clearly—that our vision isn't clouded by our emotional reactions—there's no guarantee that what we say will work.

A gentler attitude is to look at the whole process as an experiment. Do your best to come from a place of shared humanity and then experiment by saying something. In that way, we can gradually learn what works and what doesn't. But what works with Juan may not work Jasmine; or what works on Monday may not work on Wednesday. Every situation is unique. When we're dealing with other people—other complex human beings—how can we get it right every time? We can't come from a place of certainty. All we can know is that we've done our best to speak from a heart that is kind and awake.

On the bodhisattva path, there is a stage where you have a complete recognition of the true nature of reality—the wide-open, groundless, unconditioned dimension of our being. Once you have this recognition, you don't lose it—there's no going back. This stage of understanding is known as the first *bhumi*, or bodhisattva level. But the interesting thing is that after this recognition, there are nine more *bhumi*s before one attains complete enlightenment, the state of the Buddha.

When I first heard about this, I was incredulous: "*Nine more?*" Then I heard Dzigar Kongtrul Rinpoche teaching on this subject, and he said, "The other *bhumi*s are about learning how to communicate." They are deeper and deeper stages of learning how to heal: how not to polarize, but instead to help others return to their mind of open awareness, their basic goodness. Learning to speak from the heart is a long journey, but it's a journey well worth undertaking, for it brings us to a place where we can truly bring out the best in one another.

10

How You Label It Is
How It Appears

*Never underestimate the power of mind. How you
work with things really can transform what seems to be.
Working with the inner has the ability to transform
the outer—though not in any linear way you can
put your finger on.*

WHEN I BECAME DIRECTOR OF GAMPO ABBEY, THE
monastery in Nova Scotia founded by Trungpa Rinpoche, I drove everyone nuts. One of the reasons I was such
a bad director at first was I wanted everything to be aestheti-
cally pleasing according to my taste. It was especially important that everything be clean. I remember one of the monks
saying, "All you care about is clean. What about people's spiritual realization?"

The kitchen was especially bad. But no matter how much
I nagged and bought new products and made staff changes
and went in myself to show people how to clean, nothing
changed. I would even go down in the middle of the night to

organize the drawers. (I didn't want people to realize the full extent of my fussiness, but once someone caught me at two a.m., which was very embarrassing.) But two days later, I'd open a drawer and it was just as bad as before.

Finally, after going through a lot of torment, I remembered something from one of the teachings I'd studied. The great fourteenth-century yogi Longchenpa said that how we label things is how they appear to be. I decided to experiment with this teaching and see how it applied to my obsession with cleanliness. I said to myself, "I don't care if the whole place is a mess. I'm going to work on my propensity to label things in negative ways, such as 'dirty' and 'disorganized.' I'm going to pay more attention to how I project my own version of reality onto the world. I'm more interested in doing this than in having everything the way I want it to be." It was hard. I practically had to tape my mouth and tie my hands in order not to say or do anything.

Because I was only spending part of each year at the abbey, each time I came back I had a chance to see things fresh. And as the years went by, I started thinking, "This can't be true, but the kitchen is very clean and orderly. I don't have to do anything to the drawers." Instead of my whole being going into a knot of contraction, I felt relaxed and happy in there. It was a miracle.

Now I know that some people would say that I just lowered my standards. I honestly can't say for sure how much the kitchen actually got cleaner versus how much less the dirtiness bothered me. But in a way it doesn't really matter. I felt much better, which made everyone else feel less tense, which improved the atmosphere overall.

To see that how we label things is how they appear does not

mean that we stop working with outer circumstances. Often external situations do need to be changed in a concrete, reliable way. Otherwise, there would never have been any civil rights movement, or any other actions by heroic bodhisattvas who are inspired to help at the outer level. But if we don't work with our own mind and perceptions, no political or economic revolution will really change the deep habits that keep us caught in our own emotional struggles—which lead to most of our struggles with other people. If we don't notice and work with our projections, we won't be able to reduce the suffering of ourselves and others. Nor will we be able to fulfill our longing and commitment to wake up for the benefit of all living beings.

Thogme Zangpo's *Thirty-Seven Practices of a Bodhisattva* contains a series of verses that deal with how to work with difficult circumstances in your life by changing how you label them. He writes about situations that would normally feel like your worst nightmares, such as getting robbed, being shouted at unjustly, and having your beloved child turn against you. In each of these examples, he gives advice about turning the painful event into an occasion for spiritual awakening.

For example, one of the verses goes, "Even if someone humiliates you and denounces you in front of a crowd of people, think of this person as your teacher and humbly honor him." When someone treats us in such an unkind way, our natural reaction is to think of them as an enemy, along with any number of negative labels. But for the bodhisattva, this humiliator and denouncer can be a great teacher.

How could someone who torments you be your teacher? The reason is that in order to wake up, we have to learn to stop struggling with reality. In other words, we have to overcome our ego, "that which resists what is." Let's say you have a big, oozing pimple on your nose. You've figured out a way to look in the mirror without really seeing it, and when you go out, you cover the lump with cosmetics. You just can't face the fact that you have this hideous thing on your face. Then a four-year-old child marches up to you and says in front of a crowd of people, "What's that big thing on the end of your nose?" This child is giving you an up-close-and-personal look at your ego. She's showing you where you're resisting reality, where you are tight and need to loosen. In this way, you could say the child is your teacher.

Machik Labdron, a great Tibetan practitioner who lived in the eleventh and twelfth centuries, had a list of radical suggestions for getting unstuck from our ego-clinging. The first of these is "Reveal your hidden faults." Instead of concealing our flaws and being defensive when they are exposed, she counseled us to be open about them.

If you've taken a good look in the mirror, gotten over your wincing, and completely accepted the pimple just as it is, then you don't need someone else to reveal your hidden fault. You can say to the child, "Right on! Good observation!" But this response is only realistic for those who have come a long way in their practice of welcoming the unwelcome. Until we reach that stage, we will need people to point out our various "pimples" so that we get more comfortable with owning them. It doesn't have to be a major humiliation in front of a crowd. Often enough, without even meaning to, someone will say something to us that exposes a hidden shame. Having the attitude that you want to grow from everything that comes to you makes it possible to use the label "teacher" instead of "insensitive jerk" or "little brat." If your goal is inner transformation, then why not see every-thing that helps you grow—however unpleasant it seems at first—as your teacher? Why not see your "enemies" as "spir-itual friends"?

Needless to say, this isn't so easy to do. It's more like an ideal behavior, along the lines of "turn the other cheek." It's where we hope to arrive if we work with our mind and its habits over a long period of time. We can't just hear a piece of inspiring advice and immediately go from wanting to slug the person to being able to turn the other cheek. We have to work with where we are and allow a gradual transformation to happen. But to whatever degree we can implement this attitude, we will have that much strength in dealing with sit-uations that might normally cause us deep distress. We will feel that much more at ease in the world.

Never underestimate the power of mind. How you work with things really can transform what seems to be. Work-ing with the inner has the ability to transform the outer—though not in any linear way you can put your finger on. For example, if you work with your own aggression, everyone seems friendlier. I used to feel under attack all the time, but now people seem pretty nice. Is that because I have less ag-gression or because they're actually nicer? You never get to know a definite answer. But what becomes increasingly clear is that your inner work has a profound effect on how you perceive the outer world. This is why we should pay attention to how we label things.

Toward the end of my mother's life, I had developed a very unflattering view of her. I labeled this woman—who had been a really good mother to me—with words such as "hypo-chondria" and "self-pity." This was partly my reaction to some of the difficulties we were having as I began to lead a more unconventional life. Then at one point, I met an old friend of hers I'd never met before. The two of us really clicked, so we went on walks and talked a lot. She saw my mother as funny, sassy, inventive, creative—a totally different human being. I was thinking, "*Mom?*" And I realized that as I labeled her, so she appeared to me. I was fixated on just one or two facets of her, and then I met this friend who had a totally different vision. Another interesting thing was that the friend had heard a lot of bad things about me and was surprised that she genuinely liked me. We were both surprised, and both had a chance to get unstuck from our narrow labels.

Trungpa Rinpoche used the phrase "random labeling" to help us realize the arbitrariness of how we often speak and think about things. If you speak English, you use the word "chair" for the object you sit on. In Romanian, it's *scaun*. In Zulu, it's *isihlalo*. It's just a neutral object, and then we give it a label. Of course, we need language so that we are able to coexist and talk about things. It's an innocent part of human behavior. But then this strange thing happens where the object or feeling or person that we label actually *becomes* that label in our mind. We believe in our arbitrary designation.

If we get too fixated on our label, we forget that the nature of things is open, fluid, and subject to change and interpretation. When I labeled the kitchen as "dirty"—a label that had a strong emotional charge for me—it became fixed that way in my mind and colored how I actually saw it. But if we remember that labels are merely labels, we can use them to our advantage. We can use the fluid, open-to-interpretation nature of things to work with our habits.

The practice of tonglen is another way of working with our labeling. Normally, when we suffer from any kind of pain, or when we notice certain of our propensities that cast us in an unflattering light, we do everything we can to avoid those feelings. Maybe we don't consciously label them as "bad," but that's how they feel to us. With tonglen, we purposely lean into what we want to avoid and start to turn these labels around. It's not that suddenly what's "bad" becomes "good" and what's "good" becomes "bad." But we start to discover that by gradually opening up to the difficult and painful, our heart becomes warmer toward ourselves and warmer toward others.

What was formerly "bad" is transformed into bodhichitta. It becomes a longing to wake up so that we can stop causing ourselves and others pain, and instead help others realize their full potential of joy and basic goodness. The discomfort in the feeling may remain for a while, but it is no longer firmly fixed in the "bad" category. We may still feel a strong desire to reject, but as long as we keep challenging ourselves by breathing in the unwelcome, the practice will continue to open our heart.

The more we experiment with labels, the easier it becomes to see through them and to use them to our advantage. We will continue to use labels to think and communicate—but more positively, and without investing them with so much seriousness. Trungpa Rinpoche told this story about how he once was sitting in a garden with Dilgo Khyentse Rinpoche, one of his most important teachers. They were just enjoying their time together in the beautiful setting, hardly saying anything, simply happy to be there with each other. Then Khyentse Rinpoche pointed and said, "They call that a 'tree,'" and both of them roared with laughter. For me this is a wonderful illustration of the freedom and enjoyment that await us when we stop being fooled by our labels. The two enlightened teachers thought it was a riot that this complex, changing phenomenon, with all its leaves and bark and fragrance, could be thought of merely as a "tree." As our labels loosen their grip on us, we too will start to experience our world in this lighter, more magical way.

11

The Practice of Open Awareness

Practicing open awareness is a gradual process
of continually going back to seeing what we're seeing,
smelling what we're smelling, feeling what we're feeling.
Whatever happens, the method is to keep letting go
of the extra stuff and return to just what's here.

THERE'S A TANTALIZING STANZA FROM THOGME Zangpo's *Thirty-Seven Practices* that I like to contemplate from time to time. I find it very helpful because it interrupts the momentum of how I habitually see and think about the world. The stanza, in Ken McLeod's translation from his book *Reflections on Silver River*, goes like this:

> Whatever arises in experience is your own mind.
> Mind itself is free of any conceptual limitations.
> Know that and don't entertain
> Subject-object fixations—this is the practice of a
>   bodhisattva.

Now this may sound very philosophical, but it's directly related to what we've been talking about in terms of going beyond our labels. If you don't quite understand what the stanza is saying, that's good. You're probably better off than if you *think* you know. Thogme Zangpo is trying to take us beyond our usual thought processes. He is pointing to something that really can't be described or expressed. So, it's better to approach these lines with a wide-open mind than with a lot of preconceived ideas. As the Zen teacher Suzuki Roshi famously said, "In the beginner's mind, there are many possibilities, but in the expert's, there are few."

The first line of the stanza refers to our tendency to confuse how we label things with how they truly are. *Sem*, the Tibetan word translated here as "mind," refers to the conceptual mind—the mind that labels, judges, compares, concretizes, and solidifies. In other words, this line is saying we don't experience anything directly. Needless to say, this is a provocative statement. Except for during rare moments, something is always overlaying our experience—our views, our opinions, our mental and emotional pushing and pulling. For example, when we wake up in the morning, we hear rain falling on the roof. We may label the sound "soothing, relaxing, comforting." We like the sound and we want it to last. But if we'd planned a picnic or an outdoor gathering, we label the sound "bad news, threat, obstacle," and we want it to go away. In either case, however, the sound of rain remains just the sound of rain, free of all these overlays.

Sem is the mind that takes things very seriously and makes them very solid. It's what gets fixated on "me" versus "you," "us" versus "them," "this" versus "that." All our emotional reactions, all our habits, and all our karma come from this mind. You could say that *sem* creates our entire world. In reality, whatever arises in our experience is neither good nor bad, right nor wrong. Yet we spend so much energy and suffer so much because we believe in all these concepts.

The next line is "Mind itself is free of any conceptual limitations." By "mind itself," Thogme Zangpo is talking about something deeper than our labeling and concretizing mind. This is the mind of open awareness, free from fixations. When we connect to "mind itself," we experience the label-free nature of how things really are. For the sake of communication, we can still use labels such as "tree," but without confusing that label with the fluid, complex reality underneath.

Thogme Zangpo goes on to say, "Know that and don't entertain subject-object fixations." What are "subject-object fixations"? If you taste chocolate ice cream, you tend to have a sense of an "I" who is tasting. The subject (I) and the object (ice cream) are two separate things. But this separation doesn't exist in the direct experience of tasting the ice cream. In that direct experience, there is no "me" or "it." There is just taste. The separation into subject and object is a subtle form of labeling, another of the workings of *sem*.

The final part of the verse is, "This is the practice of a bodhisattva." Going beyond fixed mind and connecting with our true nature—or, in the language here, going beyond *sem* and connecting to "mind itself"—is something we can practice. Getting to know this state of open awareness is one of the most important practices on the bodhisattva path because our concepts and fixations are what bring about polarization and prevent us from fully being there for others. When we relax our mind into open awareness, we become one with our basic goodness.

There are many ways to practice open awareness, but the essence of them all is simply to show up for your life—senses open, mind and heart open—and let yourself be as free of conceptual limitations as you can be. In other words, let yourself be as free as you can from labels—"good" and "bad," "self" and "other," and all the rest. Let yourself be in this state as much as possible, according to your current level of understanding.

You can approach this practice with the attitude of "sitting in the middle of what's happening." For instance, say you're beginning an hour-long group meditation session and right away this huge anger toward someone comes up. Immediately it turns into a big issue with a storyline, full of labeling and subject-object fixations. Since you're stuck on your meditation cushion, all you can do is sit in the middle of the whole mess and, as much as possible, let go of your concepts and labels. Every time those angry thoughts come up, without repressing them you just interrupt their momentum and come back to open awareness. At the same time, you can give your big, heated issue a lot of space, so that sitting in the middle doesn't become claustrophobic. You can feel the space in your whole body, from the top of your head to the soles of your feet. Or you can go bigger, giving it the space of the room or even the vast space outside.

After sitting like this for a while, you may suddenly realize, "Where did that go?" But next thing you know, you're thinking about being criticized and you're getting worked up again. Again, you sit in the middle of it and keep letting the labeling go, with that sense of space. Eventually you find yourself again wondering, where did *that* go? As you continue through this cycle, you start to realize that your life is filled with dramas that seem to be the center of your world.

But if you keep sitting in the middle of it all, you feel it as a flow. It's not so solid anymore. It's all impermanent, and that is very good news.

This approach is similar to the practice of "just as it is." But open awareness implies an additional level of insight, which keeps unfolding over time. As we train ourselves to notice how we continually label things, we start to see how much we create our own reality. I have often found this insight to be astonishing.

This creation process starts at a very basic level. We all have a deep propensity to label things automatically—and often unconsciously—as pleasant, unpleasant, or neutral. We like it, we don't like it, or we don't care one way or the other. But "pleasant" can easily escalate into craving, crippling addiction, and all kinds of outer manifestations such as animal exploitation and the sex trade. "Unpleasant" can lead to deep-seated prejudice, hatred, and violence. And "neutral" can easily turn into indifference, being out of touch with our feelings, ignoring others, not helping people out who are in distress. All of these simple labels can manifest and escalate at the individual and the global level.

Sitting in the middle and practicing open awareness is an antidote to all these types of escalation. Because we have so many karmic seeds in our unconscious, all kinds of troubling thoughts and emotions are constantly coming up. But every time we sit with them, giving them as much space as they require, we are burning up those karmic seeds without creating new ones. Whenever the next drama pops up in your mind—whether it's a painful childhood memory or over-powering anger at your boss—if you sit in the middle of the mess and practice open awareness, you're shifting your habitual patterns. You may feel like nothing's changing, but there's a slow simmer going on. It may not be obvious, but your practice is burning up those karmic seeds, slowly but surely.

Every once in a while, you might have a more powerful insight into the profundity of open awareness. It can feel quite exhilarating, even mind-blowing. But at this stage, the experience is only a fleeting glimpse. If you try to hold on to it, if you try to get it back when it's gone, then you are going after the pleasant, rather than being with things just as they are. You are back in the realm of *sem*, the limited, conceptual mind.

Practicing open awareness is a gradual process of continually going back to seeing what we're seeing, smelling what we're smelling, feeling what we're feeling. Whatever happens, the method is to keep letting go of the extra stuff and return to just what's here. The rain in the morning isn't good or bad, comforting or threatening. It's not even "rain." It's just what it is. Everything is just what it is, beautiful yet ultimately indescribable. If we keep doing this practice—over and over, year after year, in formal meditation and in our everyday lives—we will develop unshakeable confidence that this conceptless way of being is in perfect harmony with how things really are. This will give us unshakeable confidence in our connection to others, and in our basic goodness.

12

Life Changes in an Instant

*When our bubble bursts, we can recognize that we are
walking through a very important doorway. Then we can
experiment with hanging out on the other side of that
doorway. We can learn to relax there.*

JOAN DIDION WROTE A BOOK SOME YEARS AGO CALLED
The Year of Magical Thinking. It's about the year following
an abrupt change in her life, which was her husband's unexpected death. In addition to this book's poignancy and clarity,
it also provides an accessible way of going deeper into what
it means to go beyond labeling and connect to the mind of
open awareness.

She and her husband had come back from the hospital,
where their thirty-nine-year-old daughter and only child was
in a coma and in very serious condition. They had just sat down
for a late dinner. She was focused on mixing the salad and he
was enjoying a Scotch. They were talking to each other—and
all of a sudden, he wasn't talking. He had died, just like that.

Soon after he died, she wrote something on her computer.
The next time she opened her computer, which was months

later, she read what she had written: "Life changes fast. Life changes in the instant. You sit down to dinner and life as you know it ends."

When I read these words, they resonated deeply with me. They brought to mind experiences where a sudden shock completely altered my usual, conventional, held-together view of reality. And it occurred to me that millions of people have had this kind of experience, this out-of-the-blue moment where your world completely falls apart. You don't have to be a Buddhist practitioner—I don't believe Joan Didion is one—to go through such abrupt and drastic changes to your concepts of how things are.

Dzigar Kongtrul Rinpoche talks about how all of us, whether we want to or not, live in a bubble. This is our own version of reality, created by our ego, which is always turning away from the open-ended nature of how things are and trying to maintain the familiar. Most of the time, we are able to keep this sense of familiarity intact. Everything in our bubble is fairly predictable and seems to make sense. Even if we're going through a hard time, at some level we're able to hold it all together. We get up in the morning, we enter a familiar world, we go through our day with many familiar routines. How we prepare our food, how we have our coffee, how we relate to particular people in particular ways—it's all pretty unsurprising. This isn't something we consciously choose to do. Whatever kind of life we have, we have our own version of a bubble. It's our default way of being, and most of the time, we don't even know we're doing it.

Even Joan Didion, a sophisticated woman with a rich and varied life, was living in a bubble. She knew her husband had a heart condition that might one day prove fatal.

But when she thought about the end of their time together, her thoughts would take the form of dramatic fantasies. She imagined, for example, that they'd be swimming in a cave they used to go to and the water would rise up, and they would drown together. That was "the kind of conclusion I anticipated," she wrote. "I did not anticipate cardiac arrest at the dinner table."

The first time something like this happened to me, I was also in the middle of a mundane activity. I was sitting in front of my house in New Mexico, I heard the car door slam, my husband walked around the corner, he told me he was having an affair and wanted a divorce, and—wham!—life as I knew it had ended.

I hadn't connected with the Buddhist teachings yet, so I had no frame of reference. Then, years later, I received my first teachings on *shunyata*. This Sanskrit word is most commonly translated as "emptiness." As so many people do, I at first misunderstood it. Emptiness can easily sound like a void, an absence, a state of non-existence. Some people have a notion that it's like being thrown out of a capsule in outer space and floating away for all eternity. The image I had around emptiness was like the Haunted Mansion ride at Disneyland, where the little car takes you through the house and you see all those ghostly hologram figures walking around. It took me a while to connect emptiness to what I had experienced that day in New Mexico, or to other experiences where my bubble had suddenly burst.

Nothing in our conceptual framework can prepare us for the experience of "life as you know it ends." The way our mind perceives and holds things doesn't operate anymore. All our reference points are gone; how we normally conceive of reality just doesn't work. Although she doesn't use the same language, I believe that Joan Didion is describing an experience of emptiness. It's the experience of everyone whose world falls apart in this way.

When we talk about emptiness, it's important to clarify what "empty" refers to. The word "tree" is just a convenient name for a collection of parts—trunk, limbs, leaves—that are always changing, day by day, instant by instant. We label it all as a "tree," but that label is just in our minds. In reality, there's nothing we can pin down with our limiting concepts. There's nothing permanent or solid we can hold on to. And this is true not only of trees, but of everything in the universe, including "you" and "me." Everything is empty of fixed ideas and labels. But at the same time, a tree doesn't disappear when we recognize its emptiness. We just see it more clearly as it really is: fluid, open-ended, and interconnected with everything around it.

Another way of talking about emptiness is to say that things are "free of imputed meaning." Instead of experiencing things simply as they are, our mind imputes extra layers of meaning onto them. This may sound very intellectual, but imputing meaning is something we all do, continually. For example, think about how you feel when you say "a nice cup of tea." How about "a hot shower" or "my puppy"? Do you think about the object just as it is, or is there another layer of meaning on top? To many of us, a nice cup of tea or coffee has the additional meaning of "comfort." Money in the bank can mean "security." A certain pair of shoes can mean "good taste." A spouse can mean "confirmation." But are any of these meanings actually in these objects?

When our bubble is burst by sudden events, our imputed

meanings are torn away. I read the account of a woman who was rushing to work on September 11, 2001. She was so obsessed with a presentation she had to do that she'd hardly been aware of anything else since waking up in the morning. She wasn't even sure she'd had breakfast. Her entire world was in her head. Then she walked up out of the subway station right at Ground Zero, and life as she knew it ended. One of the poignant details she wrote about was how the air was filled with paper blowing around. All those important documents and presentations had simply become loose pieces of paper floating through the air. Their imputed meanings had vanished.

Sudden experiences of emptiness can be triggered in all kinds of ways. Sometimes it's a piece of information. I knew someone who, when he was about eighteen, went through a profoundly unsettling experience after finding out he had been adopted. His adoptive parents had been very kind to him and nothing really bad had happened in his childhood, yet the discovery immediately upended the version of reality he had unknowingly constructed. Up to that point, he had lived his whole life assuming that the mother who had raised him had given birth to him and that his father had also been with him from day one. This reality was so finely integrated into his being, that when he found out the truth, he had a major experience of groundlessness. Not only were the meanings of "mother" and "father" undermined, his own very identity had come into question.

When your bubble bursts, even the most ordinary things in your life—your furniture, your neighbor, how you walk down the street—are stripped of their extra layers of imputed meaning. You find yourself in a groundless, open space. This can last for just a moment, or—in the case of a severe shock like Joan Didion's—it can last much longer. If your world is so radically upended, it may take a long time to put it back together, to get some kind of ground back under your feet.

In her book, Didion writes about how her usual routines and relationships and so forth took on a quality of meaninglessness. Though this word has a bleak connotation, when she contemplated it further, she found something more to it than bleakness. As she experienced—and as I and many others have experienced—when you have this sense of meaninglessness, you know you've connected with some kind of wisdom. You know you're onto the truth. You look out of your eyes and see the same old world, but it no longer has the fictitious meaning you imbued it with. It strikes you that, in a way, you've been making up your whole world all along. Things are just as they are, unfolding as they unfold, but our ego, continually in search of confirmation and security, imputes layer upon layer of meaning.

Often, we impute meaning in humorous ways. A few years ago, I was staying in a place with an oil stove. It looked exactly like a lovely fire in a fireplace. I enjoyed sitting in front of it, looking at the artificial logs, feeling the cozy warmth of those simulated flames. The only problem was that the oil fumes were irritating me, so I spent three days trying to outsmart the thing because I wanted that pleasant feeling of being in front of a fire without feeling sick. At some point, it occurred to me that I was behaving in this ridiculous manner just because I was imputing a meaning onto the fire—something like "home is where the hearth is." That realization cleared the way for me to be able to see how things really were. Instead of giving me pleasure, the lovely fire was giving me a splitting headache. When my bubble had burst, and I could no longer fool myself, I was able to enjoy a good laugh. Having this small insight into emptiness turned a moment of disappointment into a moment of humor.

From the Buddhist point of view, the more we get the hang of emptiness, the more delight we are open to. As we start to experience things as they really are, beyond labels and imputations, we discover a joyous freedom from our illusions. As we get to know and appreciate the open, groundless state of *shunyata*, we realize it is far more enjoyable than the fictitious "reality" we struggle so hard to maintain and improve. And discovering this leads to our having compassion for all who are engaged in that continual struggle. For this reason, developing an understanding of emptiness is one of the most important parts of the Buddhist path.

The difficulty with emptiness occurs when we have no context for understanding the experience. If emptiness is simply thrust upon us by circumstances, it can be very painful, or at least disorienting. Most people who suddenly find themselves with their imputed reality stripped away have no idea what to do. The space is too wide open and there's nothing familiar to hold on to.

We can prepare for such experiences by starting to get familiar with emptiness now. One way of doing this is the method described in the previous chapter—sitting in the middle of what's going on and letting go of concepts and labels to the best of our ability. If we do this regularly, we may, from time to time, have vivid experiences of how everything is empty of our fixed ideas and mental overlays. They can be similar to moments of "life as you know it ends," but without the shock and trauma. Although these moments of insight seem to arise from nowhere, they come about because of our practice, from our willingness to keep sitting in the middle of our karmic seeds ripening. They are the natural result of our openness and curiosity about whether our labels and mental imputations have any basis in reality.

Cultivating the experience of emptiness will give us a context for what's going on when the bottom falls out of our lives. It will give us a way of facing the most difficult and disorienting times—such as illness, loss, and eventually our own death—without so much despair and rejection. Since I started studying emptiness, I've had a few out-of-the-blue moments of having my world turned upside down. I wouldn't say the abrupt experience of having the bubble burst is fundamentally different, but having a context makes it no longer terrifying or disorienting. It doesn't give you a ground or something to hold on to, because the experience itself is one of groundlessness. But knowing about emptiness makes it possible to face it courageously. It makes it possible to appreciate the experience as something that brings us closer to the truth.

When our bubble bursts, we can recognize that we are walking through a very important doorway. Then we can experiment with hanging out on the other side of that doorway. We can learn to relax there. Eventually, we can even fall in love with emptiness, as Anam Thubten likes to say. My teachers, and the other people I've encountered who have learned to live in this open space free of imputed meaning, are the most fearless, compassionate, and joyful people I have ever known. They are living examples of what this kind of falling in love can do.

13

Cool Emptiness

*When we stop seeking the familiarity of samsara, when
we stop fighting the groundlessness of freedom from
imputed meaning, emptiness becomes an experience
of awe, of the infinite, of limitless space.*

ONCE WE BEGIN TO SEE EMPTINESS AS AN EXPERI-
ence to cultivate rather than avoid, we can take advantage of the many opportunities that arise in our lives to
learn more about it. These don't have to be sudden shocks
where the bottom falls out and we end up in freefall. Sometimes we can connect to emptiness through less dramatic
but equally unwanted emotions and states of mind. Boredom, loneliness, insecurity, uncertainty, anxiety, fear, and
even depression are all potential starting points for learning
how to go beyond our bubble of imputed meanings and
experience things just as they are.

Boredom is an experience that seems to have nothing to
offer, but it can serve as an excellent doorway to emptiness.
Trungpa Rinpoche liked to distinguish between two types
of boredom: hot and cold. Hot boredom is more familiar to

us. You're struggling against the experience. Sometimes it comes with a storyline, such as "I can't believe this is how I'm spending my precious time." Other times the story isn't so prominent. Either way, you consider the experience bad and just want to reject it. The bottom line is you want to get out of there. Cool boredom, on the other hand, starts out as basically the same experience, but instead of fighting it or running away, you allow yourself to relax with it. You open with it, and even welcome it. In other words, it's fine.

If we learn how to work with our boredom in this non-rejecting way, we can transfer that knowledge to be able to work with groundlessness. If we get the hang of experiencing boredom without struggle—learning how to relax with it and let our mind open up to appreciate its quality of spaciousness—then we can apply that skill to work with emptiness. With both run-of-the-mill hot boredom and the intensity of "life as you know it ends," there is a similar tendency to try to block or avoid our experience by getting some kind of ground under our feet. By training in cool boredom, we train in accepting things as they are. This helps us wean ourselves from the habit of closing down into our soothing world of familiar, imputed meanings.

Working with loneliness is similar. When people talk about feeling lonely, they're generally talking about hot loneliness. You feel restless. You want to find someone to talk to or be with. You feel like something's wrong. The struggle continues until you solve the problem from the outside. Cool loneliness, on the other hand, starts out in the same way, but you're able to let go of the restlessness and the struggle. With cool loneliness, you become relaxed and can enjoy the present moment. There's not the same gloomy storyline. Because you're open to the experience, you sense its fleeting nature, so you don't feel so stuck.

Insecurity, uncertainty, fear, and most other unwanted emotions each have their hot version and their cool version. Because we're much more used to the hot versions, we consider these emotions highly unpleasant—things to avoid. But this very struggle to avoid is what keeps them hot. In the cool versions, we feel more peaceful and awake. Instead of a struggle to get ground under our feet, there's a willingness—even a joyfulness—to be with things just as they are.

Even depression, which is something most of us fear, can be an excellent training ground for learning how to connect with the open, spacious quality of emptiness. One of the common effects of depression is that things lose their former meaning. That nice cup of tea just doesn't do it for you anymore. Getting that presentation for work to the next level doesn't have the overwhelming significance it used to have. You are in a groundless space where many of your reference points have vanished.

The first time my life as I knew it ended—on that long-ago day in New Mexico—I entered a period of deep depression. I can remember sitting on a couch for a whole day, almost catatonic. Even when I felt hunger pangs, they didn't have their former imputed meaning. I knew that sensation was supposed to mean I should eat something, but I was too depressed to get up.

The experience catapulted me into a whole new place in my life. For a long time, the main way I dealt with that unfamiliar, groundless feeling was by kicking and screaming, but eventually I was able to shift my view a little. Though the sensation of depression stayed the same, I was able to gain some distance from it. Then at some point, I was able to learn what the experience had to teach me. Painful experiences, including depression, have something very rich in them to offer us.

When we start to feel intimations of meaninglessness, as almost all of us do, we have a chance to shift our view. When the depression is somewhat mild—before it fully gets its claws in you and turns into an incapacitating state of mind—you can think of the discomfort you're going through as hot depression. And from that perspective, you can at least entertain the idea that it's possible to experience cool depression.

It seems odd to call depression "hot" because it doesn't feel very juicy or hot at all, but the basic feeling is "I want this to go away" or "This is something horrible." So instead of following that habitual reaction, we could think, "Maybe I could experience this depression from a cool perspective, or at least be curious about the possibility of really tasting this groundlessness." If we do this without pushing ourselves too hard, if we are gentle and warm toward ourselves in this process, then maybe we can experience depression as a doorway to the wisdom of emptiness. We could experiment with staying with the unwelcome feeling for tiny bites. Even if they last only two and a half seconds, each of those bites will help us get to know emptiness a little better, until emptiness becomes less frightening for us.

Gradually, our relationship with emptiness will go from hot to cool, and we will discover how much enjoyment and freedom is to be found in the wide-open state that exists outside our habitual bubble. When we stop seeking the familiarity of samsara, when we stop fighting the groundlessness of freedom from imputed meaning, emptiness becomes an experience of awe, of the infinite, of limitless space.

However, even if we do find ourselves attracted to or curious about emptiness, we can't simply will ourselves to live without imputed meaning. We can't just say, "Oh, I'm going to see the view out my window without imputed meaning." It's impossible because we're so locked into how we habitually see things. This habit goes deeper than we know. But when boredom, loneliness, depression, and other unwanted feelings arise, we can use them to help wean ourselves from imputed meaning. Every time we turn in the direction of inquiry and exploration—as opposed to struggle and running away—we are dismantling the whole way we impute meaning onto things. If we do this long enough, our bubble of ego will naturally wear thin, without any extra effort on our part. The true nature of how things are will become more and more available to us.

14

Experiencing Nowness

*Whenever we are between here and there, whenever
one thing has ended and we're waiting for the next thing
to begin, whenever we're tempted to distract ourselves or
look for an escape route, we can instead let ourselves
be open, curious, tentative, vulnerable.*

WHEN I AM GIVING A TEACHING ABOUT EMPTINESS
or open awareness and I want to help the audience
come to some direct experience on the spot, I sometimes
ask everyone to stand up with me. We all breathe in at the
same time and raise our hands above our heads. Then, we all
breathe out together and let our arms fall so that our hands
slap down on our thighs. I've done this with as many as six
hundred people. It can be extremely loud.

This exercise creates an opportunity for people to experi-
ence a moment of openness free from labels and imputations.
After the slap, we just relax our mind, as much as we can.
Whatever happens next is just fine. Some people experience
a gap of wide-open space. Some start talking to themselves.
Some become sad or irritated or drowsy. Some think, "I

don't get this." But whatever happens is no problem. There doesn't have to be a special experience. The main thing is for people to be open, with the relaxed attitude of allowing anything to occur, without rejection or value judgment. The loud slap creates an opportunity for a gap in our conceptual process, but if one doesn't experience that gap, there is nothing to be worried about. It is a profound practice just to let things be.

If you see emptiness as something desirable to cultivate— or even fall in love with—you can always find ways to connect with it in your everyday life. One easy way to practice emptiness is just to pause. You can do this whenever you remember. It's very simple. Slow down and abruptly stop. Look out, and touch in with the present moment. Doing so breaks up the stream of concepts and mental chatter that overlay your experience. It enables you to touch in with the timelessness of the present moment—what Trungpa Rinpoche so skillfully called "nowness."

When we're going through our busy days and irritating delays are imposed on us, we can take advantage of the situation by doing this pause practice. For instance, you're on your lunch break and you have to go to the post office. You find yourself in a long line that doesn't move. Instead of just standing there and seething, you can drop the chatter, relax, and touch in with the present moment. Then the post office and the people in it may turn into a fascinating experience. You can actually see what's before your eyes and hear what's coming into your ears. It's as if the doors of perception have been cleansed. A moment ago, you were caught up, stewing, or bored out of your mind, and now your experience is transformed into something vivid and wondrous. You are free from concepts such as "poor me" or "I don't have time for this" and are instead enjoying nowness.

I've heard that in Tibet in the past, the only way women could attain enlightenment was by practicing in the gaps of their busy and full lives. But they were so committed to awakening that they learned to recognize and appreciate the many opportunities that came their way. Any moment of "betweenness"—waiting for someone, walking from one place to another, milking a cow—became a valuable chance. Instead of thinking about what just happened or planning what would happen next, they enjoyed the space to pause the conceptual mind and touch in with nowness.

We have many similar chances in our own lives. Whenever we are between here and there, whenever one thing has ended and we're waiting for the next thing to begin, whenever we're tempted to distract ourselves or look for an escape route, we can instead let ourselves be open, curious, tentative, vulnerable.

It is possible to connect with the nowness in the times that we lose our bearings, in the times that we feel off balance. These are the times when you're uncertain about what to do and what the effects of your actions will be. This often comes about when you're having trouble making an important decision. You don't know whether to accept a job offer, or where you should move, or what medical advice you should follow. You want to help someone in need, but you don't know how. You're not sure whether it's time to take a risk or to play it safe. Or maybe it's just a minor dilemma, such as what you should wear or what you should order on the menu.

In all these cases, you would like to come to a concrete conclusion, but there is no way to arrive at anything definite.

As a result, you feel vulnerable and groundless. But if you pay attention and stay present in these situations, you can find an opportunity to touch in with the wisdom of nowness—with the open-ended, unpredictable quality of how things always are.

Once I attended a talk at Gampo Abbey by Khenchen Thrangu Rinpoche, the abbot of the monastery. When he stopped speaking, one of the monks rang a gong to signify the end of the teaching. Although that is the custom at Gampo Abbey, Thrangu Rinpoche thought the gong indicated the beginning of a meditation session. So for the next hour and a half, he sat on his cushion, totally relaxed, shifting his weight from time to time. We audience members weren't exactly sure what was happening, so we also sat there the whole time, in a state of not knowing. Was he waiting for us to end or were we waiting for him? Each of us must have had our own way of being in that situation—from relaxing with the ground-lessness to wanting to shout out—but witnessing Thrangu Rinpoche's ease gave me a deep appreciation for how one can become comfortable with nowness—with emptiness in everyday life.

In the Zen tradition, teachers make use of koans, which are questions that have no answers—at least according to fixed mind and dualistic thinking. Perhaps the most famous Zen koan is "What is the sound of one hand clapping?" This may sound like a highly esoteric practice, but if we are tuned in to the way things really are in this world—free from imputed meaning and impossible to pin down—we will notice that life continually presents us with koans.

For most of us, such times of ambivalence are negative experiences that we tend to run away from. But for spiritual practitioners, these koans can be means by which we wake up and realize the full potential of our hearts and minds. Instead of immediately trying to answer the open-ended questions that life presents us, we could experiment with relaxing with this feeling of ambivalence, if only for just a moment.

But even when life isn't handing us opportunities of groundlessness and vulnerability, we can still find ways of connecting with everyday emptiness—connecting with nowness. One practice that I especially like is taking mental snapshots. You can begin by closing your eyes. Then turn your head in any direction—up, down, sideways. It doesn't matter which way. The idea is that you're not exactly sure what you'll see when you open your eyes. Then, abruptly open your eyes and see what's in front of you. Almost immediately, you will revert to labeling everything, but try to observe that moment before the labeling happens. In a relaxed and open way, try to take a mental snapshot of that instant, which is empty of imputed meaning.

You can do this throughout the day, wherever you are. You don't necessarily have to close your eyes first, but that can help you get the hang of the practice. If you're a photographer or another type of artist, this kind of activity may well feel natural, but try to adapt it as an emptiness practice—a way to connect with nowness. You can also do this practice with other perceptions. For instance, you can suddenly become aware of the sounds you are hearing and try to observe that moment before you identify them and decide whether you like them or not.

The snapshot practice gives us an insight into the mind of a meditator who has gained experience in seeing things as they are. For such a person, there is a continual feeling of surprise. You're surprised that things are not the way you thought they were—or for that matter, that they *are* the way you thought they were. This is the fresh, unconventional perception of the artist-meditator. Trungpa Rinpoche, who taught us this snapshot practice, was passionately involved with the arts. His photographs are very interesting. There's one that shows on one side the last two letters of a huge gas station sign. Then there's a big space, and in the opposite corner of the photo are the first two letters of another sign. It all comes together as this beautiful, timeless moment.

All these practices of everyday emptiness are about connecting to the freshness of each moment. For young children, that freshness is much more available. But it is available for adults as well. Sometimes that freshness is thrust upon us, as in the case of a sudden shock. Other times we have to cultivate it intentionally. But however we get there, the idea is to value these moments as glimpses of a greater truth that lies behind our habitual labeling. If we keep seeking out and taking advantage of these opportunities, our nervous system will increase its capacity to hold uncertainty, ambiguity, and insecurity. If we continue to venture out of our comfort zone and increase our tolerance for such feelings, our lives will change. Instead of feeling like we have to wear armor to defend ourselves as we go through our days, it will feel more as if we're watching a movie. One of the great results of practicing this way is that we feel like we have nothing to lose.

15

Birth and Death in Every Moment

Birth and death, birth and death—they keep going on and on, continually and eternally. As we become more accustomed to this flow, we start seeing things in a fresh way.

WHEN WE BEGIN TO EXPLORE EMPTINESS, WE SET foot in a world beyond the bubble of our fixed ideas and labels. We begin to get in tune with the fluid, elusive nature of how things really are. In many ways, it's easy to appreciate the wonder and beauty of this reality. Day turns into night and back into day, the moon waxes and wanes, the seasons go through their dramatic and subtle changes. When a flower blooms and then starts to fade, we accept the poignancy of that change. Even if the decay of the flower makes us sad, we can appreciate it as part of the movement of life. Imagine what it would be like if things existed in a fixed way. Wouldn't life get boring pretty fast?

In Buddhist teachings, however, the subject of impermanence invariably leads to the "D-word." For most of us, thinking about death is not within our comfort zone. The inevitability of our own death and the deaths of our loved ones isn't as easy to accept as the changing of the seasons. This is especially the case if we live in a culture where death is usually kept hidden, which is how it is in much of the Western world.

When I was in my thirties, I lived with my family in a small village in Mexico. The attitude to death was very different there from what I was used to. There wasn't such a need to hide it away. For instance, when a baby died, the little coffin would be carried through the town on someone's head. Of course, the people in the village would be very sad and miss their loved ones when they died. They weren't disconnected from their feelings. But there wasn't an attitude of, "No, no! This should not be happening." When our family walked from where we lived to the plaza, we would pass a funeral home where the bodies of the dead were clearly visible through a big window. One day my children were late getting home. They said they'd taken a big detour to avoid seeing the dead bodies. But by the time we left, they were more comfortable with seeing death and we had all became more familiar with such sights.

I've observed a number of people die. When they've made a relationship to death, they're usually able to let go and make the transition more easily. But if they're afraid of death, it can be painful to watch. You see a terror in their eyes as if they're being pushed into a deep pit. Having witnessed both of these kinds of death, I know which way I want to go. This has been a very important inspiration for me to keep contemplating death. Now, having worked with it for a long time, I no longer see death as frightening. And I've started to teach more about death because I feel that being so afraid of it is really unnecessary.

Recently I started doing a practice that has helped me deepen my own relationship with death. It came out of a conversation I had with Anam Thubten Rinpoche. "This morning I was with my friend," he told me.

> We were in an art store buying brushes, ink, and paper so we could do calligraphy together. Now that memory is like a past lifetime. It's over forever and will never happen like that again. It came into being, lasted a while, and then was finished, never to return. And now I'm here with you. We're talking, there's this table between us, there are pictures on the wall, and we're in this space together. Then this experience will be over. It'll be another memory. It'll pass away and never be the same again. And you and I both will be in another lifetime. This morning was like a past lifetime, our conversation now will soon be another past lifetime, and then there'll be another lifetime after that. Things are continuously being born and ceasing. And it will keep going like that in a continuous flow for all of eternity.

We usually think of birth and death in terms of the whole cycle this body goes through, which can take place over many decades. But every day, we go through continual cycles of birth and death. Every event of our lives has a beginning, a middle, and an end. First, it comes into being; it is born. Then it ends; it dies. And in between these births and deaths, there are many smaller moments with their own births and deaths. Every day is made of countless moments, and each of these precious moments ends and becomes a past lifetime.

I took what Anam Thubten told me and decided to try it out as a practice. I think of this as an exercise in recognizing birth and death in every moment. I've also recommended this to many people, and the feedback I've received suggests that many who do this practice will eventually lose their fear of death. It makes death become so familiar that it stops feeling threatening.

The practice is very simple. Recollect an event or a moment from yesterday or earlier today. Contemplate how it is gone forever, like a past lifetime. Just keep doing this, over and over again. Do it whenever you think of it—when you wake up in the morning, when you can't sleep at night, just whenever it occurs to you. If you keep up with this practice regularly—if you keep it current—you'll begin to get a feeling of stepping into the flow of impermanence. You'll experience directly how nothing exists in a fixed way. Birth and death, birth and death—they keep going on and on, continually and eternally.

As we become more accustomed to this flow, we start seeing things in a fresh way. We notice the uniqueness of each moment. Say you're sitting somewhere with this book right now. There are sounds and smells—some natural, some unnatural. The light and the air have their own fleeting and subtle qualities. Your body is going through many sensations—heat, cold, tightness, relaxation, and so on. Each moment is like its own vignette, and each vignette fades into the past, never to return.

In all of these experiences, there appears to be someone who experiences them. This is "you," the person who has your name. But as you contemplate birth and death in every moment, you start to realize that "you" and "I" have no fixed identities. This morning's breakfast, last night's phone call, yesterday's errand—every vignette you have lived through is experienced by "you," but that "you" keeps changing. The main character in one scene goes away, to be replaced by the main character of the next scene. It's a different "you" in every scene. Even the "you" that began reading this chapter is no longer here. You and I are continually dissolving and regrouping, continually experiencing death and rebirth.

Thich Nhat Hanh, who has such a poetic way of putting things, talks about how our body is like a river. All the cells are like drops of water that are continually bubbling up and disappearing. And our minds, with all their ephemeral perceptions, thoughts, and feelings, are exactly the same way. We may identify with our values or our opinions or our personality, but these are all continually changing. There is no aspect of "me" or "you" that doesn't undergo a continual flow of birth and death. This will gradually dawn on us as we keep experimenting with this practice.

As you get more familiar with birth and death in every moment, you will discover other benefits. You will have the insight that there are continual and endless opportunities to have a fresh start. In each new moment, one lifetime ends, and another begins. This means you always have another chance. You can never be stuck. For instance, something comes up and your habitual reaction is to feel insecure. Then you think, "I'm insecure. I'm an insecure person. That's who I am." But an hour later, you're not having that experience of insecurity. It's as if you're no longer the same "insecure person." That moment has died and is part of a past lifetime. So has the person who experienced that moment of insecurity. Now you have another chance. And if you again revert to feeling insecure, you have another chance—and another chance after that. You can do the same habitual thing ump-teen times, you can even blow it completely, but there's no end to the number of fresh starts you get. There's no fixed "you" doomed to stay in the same rut forever. In this way, the death that happens every moment is a great blessing.

There is a traditional Tibetan mind training slogan that reads, "Regard all dharmas as dreams." Trungpa Rinpoche reworded this as "See everything as a passing memory." When we practice recognizing birth and death in every mo-ment, this becomes our natural way of seeing. Nothing that happens in our lives is more fixed or solid than a passing memory. If we can begin to actually experience this, it will enrich our lives and our deaths immensely.

16

Imagine Life without Ego

The Dharma often speaks of overcoming the ego and even attaining an irreversible state of egolessness, but to many of us this just sounds like a theory. It almost seems like the teachings are referring to a plane of existence that lies somewhere beyond our human world. But overcoming ego is something that any of us can do.

"YOU HAVE DIVORCED YOUR HUSBAND AND NOW YOU should divorce Pema Chödrön." I received this cryptic message a few summers ago from Anam Thubten Rinpoche. When I asked him what he meant, he said it was just a silly message and didn't elaborate. But later, when I was doing a meditation retreat, I had an insight into what I think he was getting at.

Lifetime after lifetime, I've been born and been given a name, and lifetime after lifetime I've identified completely with that persona. It dawned on me what a waste that has been. What a waste to keep getting tricked in the same way, and to keep missing chance after chance to experience the profound relaxation of being with things just as they are.

Like all sentient beings, I have an ongoing, moment-by-moment experience. My five senses experience sights, sounds, smells, tastes, and tactile sensations, and my mind experiences thoughts and emotions. This is not a problem at all. It's what being alive is like—an amazing and wondrous blessing.

But the sad part is that I've kept identifying myself as the one who experiences all this. This has turned into the illusion of a continuous, fixed, separate entity, which for the last few decades I've thought of as "Pema Chödrön." With this feeling of a solid, unchanging experiencer, I've become stuck—yet again. I've found myself in this situation where it's Pema Chödrön "against" her experience, or Pema Chödrön "for" her experience, or Pema Chödrön "indifferent" to her experience. And from these three basic reactions, all kinds of intense emotions, harmful actions, and painful results arise.

As I continued with the contemplation, I asked myself what I could do differently this time around. How can I divorce this Pema Chödrön? Is it even possible to do so? What would it look like to go on living and experiencing and functioning, but without identifying with any fixed persona? Or, to use more Buddhist terminology, what would it look like to live without ego?

The Dharma often speaks of overcoming the ego and even attaining an irreversible state of egolessness, but to many of us this just sounds like a theory. It almost seems like the teachings are referring to a plane of existence that lies somewhere beyond our human world. But overcoming ego is something that any of us can do.

The reason why it's possible to live without ego is because ego is a false identity. Pema Chödrön happens to be my name, but it's not who I am. I have many other labels—"teacher," "nun," "American," "old lady," and so on—but none of these are who I am. There is no way to sum up a person in a name, or a few words, or even a few volumes of words. Our names and labels serve the practical purpose of helping us to conceptualize and communicate, but they are not who we are. The way to go beyond ego is to stop believing in these empty identities.

Even enlightened people still have a sense of being. They have a sense of inhabiting a body—a particular body that's old or young, male or female, tall or short, dark or light. But what they don't have is a sense of belonging to or identifying with their body or their persona. They can do things without identifying with a doer, they can have experiences without a fixed experiencer, they can have thoughts without a thinker.

This way of being may sound foreign, but you can experiment with it and get a sense of what it's like. For instance, when you eat, contemplate what it would mean to eat without an eater. When you move, explore moving without a mover. When you see or hear, ask yourself what it would be like to do it without a see-er or hearer. When you meditate, look into doing it without a meditator. Whatever you do, try to have a sense of phenomena just unfolding without the presence of a person reacting to or trying to control the experience. This is along the lines of Thogme Zangpo's advice not to "entertain subject-object fixations." Whatever you do, see if you can experience it directly, without any separation between who you are and what you're doing.

There's no guarantee about what you'll discover through this experiment, but you might find yourself connecting to a free, nonconceptual experience of just eating, just walking, or whatever it is, without this feeling of *me*, the eater, the walker. When this happens, you are getting the flavor of what it's like to live without ego.

The difference between living with and without ego is like the difference between static and fluid. Because ego's tendency is to resist the open-ended, empty nature of how things are, when our experience is dominated by ego, our perceptions become frozen and lose their vibrancy.

When I was young, I had a very interesting dream, which has remained vivid in my memory to this day. I was in a fluid state without any sense of opposition—no "me" against "you," or "me" against anything. There was just a wide-open feeling that felt dynamic and alive. The word that kept coming to my mind was "process." I recognized how everything was in process—moving, growing, living. I had a deep sense of what it was to be me and what it was to be in interchange with everything my senses perceived. And I had the thought: "Nothing is like it seems to be." I recognized how the fixed, solid way I usually perceived things was just an illusion.

When I woke up, it was so shocking. I opened my eyes, and suddenly there I was, back in this frozen world. My sense perceptions were back to seeing everything in a fixed way. It felt like everything was made of plastic, like that plastic sushi they display outside some Japanese restaurants. I remember finding this very depressing. I'd had an experience of something that felt like the truth, but there was no way for me to get back there.

Years later, when I started hearing Buddhist teachings on emptiness and egolessness, I used that dream as a reference point. It resonated with the words that Trungpa Rinpoche and other teachers used—"dynamic," "fluid," "in process," "alive." But these teachers not only gave me a sense of what the experience of egolessness felt like; they pointed the way to how I could gradually cultivate freedom from ego.

If ego is such a big problem, it would seem that the most natural solution is to get rid of it. Isn't it like when you have someone in your office or community or family who's a huge pain in the neck? You want to get rid of that person, or at least you wish you somehow never had to see them or deal with them again. That's a normal response to difficulty. And with all the teachings about how the ego is the biggest troublemaker in our lives—the biggest pain in the neck— why would we not just try to get rid of it?

However, the idea that we need to get rid of ego is a misunderstanding, one that many people—even experienced Buddhist practitioners—share. The notion that we need to get rid of something within ourselves is a setup for intensifying our inner struggle. It can only inflame our tendency to be unfriendly to ourselves. What the Buddha taught instead is the method of non-rejection.

Instead of getting rid of ego, the idea is to become very conscious of ego and how it works. Only by getting to know ego intimately will it lose its power to keep us spinning in samsara. Ego manifests in all the countless ways we resist what is. It is there in all our pushing away what we don't want and pulling in what we do want. It shows its face in all our solid views, opinions, and fixed ideas. It is present in the ways we identify ourselves, such as "weak," "strong," "broken," "wise," "competent," "unworthy," and so on.

The heart of the practice is to notice all of this and rest in the middle of it all, not trying to fix or alter anything. Whatever arises, we can practice just being there with as much ease, curiosity, and openness as possible. We can work on no-ticing and experiencing all this activity of our minds—doing nothing with it beyond simply noticing.

Our journey toward living without ego is to learn how to let go, relax, take a chance, wait and see, and never sum our-selves up. This is our path, which we can keep working on every day, to the best of our current ability. This is what I've set out to do for myself, in my effort to divorce Pema Chödrön. It's a friendly divorce and one that I know will take a while. But for sure, I don't want to waste another lifetime taking this current, very fleeting, very fragile persona so seriously.

17

Our Wisdom Changes
the World

Whether distraction and aggression proliferate globally or
peacefulness and harmony grow stronger depends on how
we as citizens of the world feel about ourselves.

WE CAN'T HAVE AN ENLIGHTENED SOCIETY OR A sane and peaceful world if the individuals within it are stuck in small, fixed mind. Out of our individual ability to connect with big mind and big heart—in other words, with our basic goodness—we can manifest a culture where people care for themselves and care for each other. We can have a society where we see each other's potential, rather than seeing each other as broken or messed up.

For most of us, this is a work in progress. I may see four people's basic goodness and potential, but then there's someone who really gets under my skin and I think, "About this one, I'm not so sure!" And sadly, sometimes you yourself are the one whose basic goodness you doubt the most.

This kind of deficient self-image is especially prevalent in our culture. I don't like to idealize the Tibetan culture but one thing I've heard and observed is that Tibetan people don't question whether their underlying basic nature is good. For instance, if someone notices he has jealousy, he doesn't think, "This means I'm intrinsically jealous" or "This proves I'm a bad person." He sees it more as a temporary and removable habitual pattern. The jealousy has to be grappled with, but it's not a permanent aspect of his character.

When His Holiness the Dalai Lama started meeting with Buddhist teachers from the West, they would tell him how their students often expressed self-denigration. Even the teachers often had negative views of themselves. For the Dalai Lama, at first, these words just didn't compute. Having a bad self-image was completely alien to how he saw himself and others. It was so far away from the open-ended and basically good nature that he knew everyone possessed. It didn't make sense that people could be so hard on themselves, so judgmental—even to the point of self-hatred.

Somebody once asked the Dalai Lama how one could maintain the view of basic goodness when there was so much evil in the world. He responded by talking about very little children, who are almost always kind and considerate, open and generous. This goes along with some studies I've heard about that investigate how toddlers relate to the world. When shown pictures of other children being happy or kind, say to little animals, the toddlers smile and laugh. But when they see pictures of unkindness or children getting hurt, they become unhappy. These findings demonstrate that in early life, before a lot of fixed ideas become entrenched, the quality of basic human nature is loving. The Dalai Lama explained that as we grow up, secondary causes arise that obscure our loving, open nature. For example, when we reach adolescence a lot of our past karma ripens in a way that often results in confusion. But these obscurations are only temporary, like clouds moving in on a clear day and blocking the sun. Our basic goodness isn't gone and doesn't have to be re-created. We just need to apply effective methods to uncover it.

To work with this, I've found it is really helpful to practice intentionally contacting basic goodness. In some way, the point of doing this is to help me connect with the unbiased open space that's always available to all of us. But at the same time, the point is to see very clearly what blocks us from connecting with the openness of our being. Instead of just focusing on the sun, we also acknowledge the clouds that obscure the sun. If we try to focus on our basic goodness, but we feel like there's basically something wrong with us, then the practice will be ineffective and most likely unproductive. It's like waking up to an overcast cloudy day and saying the sun isn't shining. But of course, the sun is always shining. It is never gone away. We need to become familiar with the clouds, and if we get really intimate with them, we will see how insubstantial they are. Their density and solidity fall apart, and we see that the sun of wisdom has never stopped shining. And that clarity and warmth is available to us always.

The feeling of "something's inherently wrong with me" is one of the most important clouds for us to get intimate with. Here is one approach. Close your eyes and look within to see if you can contact that deficient feeling. Sometimes it helps to recall an instance where that feeling came up strongly for you. Something happened or was said that triggered your habit of feeling bad about yourself. Bringing up that memory can help you connect to the feeling.

Now ask yourself a couple questions. The first is, "Does this feeling depend on an internal dialogue, a story line?" In other words, if you go beneath the words of the story, is the feeling still there? And the second question is, "What would it mean for me personally to accept this feeling with kindness? What would it mean for me just to let it be?"

The first question is important because, if we don't make the effort to go beneath the words, the dialogue has a tendency to keep talking away, wanting to solve it or wanting to make us feel worse about ourselves. We try to find the simplicity of the whole thing, without all the spinoff, without turning up the fire by escalating the storyline.

It all can become much simpler, but is the feeling still there? When I first started experimenting with this, I remember thinking that if I dropped the storyline there wouldn't be anything underneath. It seemed like quite an insight to discover that even without all the words the negative feeling was indeed still there. It was there, but in a preverbal form. For instance, if I brought up this feeling by thinking about what someone said to me, even when I went beneath my internal dialogue, there would still be some kind of preverbal negative energy I could feel.

Once you contact that preverbal feeling or energy, the next thing is to stay there, without spinning off, and look at it with tenderness. I like the wording "What would it mean for me personally to fully accept this feeling; to not reject it but embrace it?" This is something we have to figure out for ourselves. A teacher or a book can advise you to accept something or let it be, and that can make sense to you in a conceptual way, but how do you actually do it? For me, the approach to acceptance can be found in this Shambhala saying: "Place the fearful mind in the cradle of loving-kindness." In other words, be friendly to yourself.

You can't be friendly and judgmental at the same time. If you have a good friend, you probably know all about her strangeness. You probably have some ideas about how she could be happier if she went about some things a little differently. But if you do call her out on her issues, you don't do it in a harsh, critical way. You don't do it out of thinking there's something inherently wrong with her. You do it out of your care. You do it because you think it will help her see what's going on, which will help her get over her negative habits. And if she recognizes where you're coming from, she may tell you to go away, but underneath there's a good chance she'll appreciate what you're saying.

This is the kind of friendly approach we can gradually learn to have toward ourselves and our uncomfortable feelings. It will enable us to stay with the feeling beneath the words long enough for us to become intimate with it. The preverbal energy may persist, but we will develop a different relationship to it. It won't automatically turn into "something's wrong with me" and the whole internal conversation that follows.

Accepting something, by the way, isn't the same as *liking* it. To accept a feeling that we habitually associate with discomfort doesn't mean we immediately turn around and start enjoying it. It means being okay with it as part of the texture of human life. It means understanding that, if we want to become fully awakened human beings, we have to learn how not to shy away from or reject any human experience. It's like accepting the weather. We may prefer sunny to rainy, or spring to winter, but fundamentally we accept the way the weather and the seasons are.

So personally, I've made a commitment to keep pointing myself toward changing how I look at myself and how I look at other people. It starts with getting in touch with the feeling of something being wrong with me and then making the intention to work with loosening that feeling up by seeing it with tenderness. Eventually I've learned how I can just let it be. If each of us can change how we look at ourselves, that becomes the basis for a culture of people who don't give up on themselves or on each other. And this is something that we certainly need now more than ever.

I think it's even fair to say that how we feel about ourselves will determine the future of the world. Whether distraction and aggression proliferate globally or peacefulness and harmony grow stronger depends on how we as citizens of the world feel about ourselves.

Trungpa Rinpoche emphasized that we are at a crossroads. As we see, there is so much violence, polarization, environmental degradation, and suffering all over the globe. Things seem like they're spinning out of control. We can respond to this state of affairs with fear, aggression, and selfishness, or we can respond out of trust in our vast, open, basically good mind, which is timelessly aware, yet empty of imputed meanings. How we respond will determine the way the world will go. As citizens of our world, we can help things go in the direction of wisdom, caring, and compassion.

18

Welcoming the Unwelcome
with Laughter

Humor lightens up the spiritual path and prevents it
from becoming a drag. It gives us the openness to go
deeper into the teachings, rather than become fixated
on what we think they mean.

SOME YEARS AGO, I WAS STAYING WITH MY SON
Edward and his family. I was in their dining room and
realized I had misplaced my water bottle. As my friends and
family will tell you, I tend to fret and obsess over the tiniest
things. So, I started searching everywhere, like a little mouse.
"Is it under here? Is it on top of this? Is it inside this bag?
Where is it? Where is it? Oh, I think I left it at the mall! Could
we call the mall?"

My son had just read his first Buddhist book because his
daughter had given it to him. Observing my neurotic behavior, which I wasn't really conscious of, he took the opportunity to poke fun at his Buddhist nun mother. He said to his
son Pete, who was then around twelve, "See what grandma's

doing there? She's suffering. And you know why she's suffering, Pete? Because she's attached to that water bottle. If she just gave up her attachment to the water bottle, she would not be suffering anymore." I said, "Pete, your father sure got that right!"

My son's humor cut right through my habit in a powerful way. I stopped fretting right there. I said, "You know, who cares if I ever find that water bottle. I want to work with this pattern of fretting." And everyone in the family said, "Yay!" Even now, when I start obsessing over something, I often remember this incident. Having a good laugh at myself helps me to drop it.

All of my teachers have had a great sense of humor and have valued humor as an important part of the spiritual path. It is a key part of being friendly to ourselves. Many of us go through our days haunted by our imperfection. We think there's something fundamentally wrong with us. Some people react to this feeling by making themselves busy all the time—rushing around frantically, with a high level of stress. Some dull themselves with substances and other forms of escape. Some simply become very dour. But all these are ways of escaping the dreadful feeling that we are somehow not okay. When we laugh at ourselves, on the other hand, all our terrible flaws become less solid and serious.

I have a friend who sometimes sends me humorous cards with spiritual themes. One of them shows an angry bald man in Buddhist monks' robes throttling another Buddhist monk. The caption says, "Having an Unbuddha-like Moment?" Another shows a woman sitting in the half-lotus position and has the caption, "Here I sit, totally evolved and at one with all life . . . compassionately not judging stoopid people."

These are thoughts no "proper Buddhist" should think. It seems very Unbuddha to secretly rejoice when your friend fails, or to fish for compliments, or to be obsessed about a water bottle. We may feel like we're the only one among our spiritual companions who feels arrogant or lustful or pessimistic. Jarvis Masters told me he doesn't like it when chaplains and other helpers—Buddhist or not—come in to the prison with big smiles on their faces and preach about virtue and ethics and always looking on the bright side. He said, "I start to feel, 'Am I the only one having a bad thought here?'"

But having these "bad thoughts" gives us the perfect occasion to laugh at ourselves. Even when we make sincere aspirations every day to wake up for the benefit of all sentient beings, countless habitual thoughts can still arise in our minds. The truth is that almost all of us could be the subject of our own book of Unbuddha cartoons. But without humor, it will be hard to have enough patience and resilience to face the steady stream of painful and incriminating thoughts and feelings that come up. We will feel like we're surrounded by enemies: our petty desires, our unexpected prejudices, our constant complaining. Instead, if we take ourselves less seriously, we can view these unwelcome mental arisings as old friends. If you find yourself obsessing over a water bottle, you can think, "Oh, there you are again, my old, familiar friend, Neurotic Fretting."

Being able to laugh at ourselves connects us with our humanness. This in turn helps us connect to and have empathy with other people. We realize how all of us are fundamentally equal. We all have our natural goodness as well as plenty of bothersome and neurotic habits. If we scorn and criticize ourselves for our weaknesses, we'll inevitably scorn and criticize others. But if we appreciate ourselves just as we are, without judgment, it will be that much easier to do the same in regard to others. Then it will be natural to want the best for others and to work to wake up on their behalf. For this reason, humor is considered to be one of the indispensable qualities of the spiritual path.

Humor lightens up the spiritual path and prevents it from becoming a drag. It gives us the openness to go deeper into the teachings, rather than become fixated on what we *think* they mean. For instance, Buddhist teachers often warn us about wasting time. There are many contemplations about how rare and precious it is to have a human life with the opportunity to practice the Dharma. But if you approach this topic without a sense of humor, you'll probably find yourself tortured by the fact that you regularly blow it. You may go to a party and be so uptight about maintaining your mindfulness that you're actually closed off to the people around you. You're so serious about not being frivolous that you start to look down on other people. The key to not wasting your life is to find a balance that includes humor—carefully applying yourself on the spot when you start getting emotionally reactive, but maintaining a sense of lightness and playfulness.

The Buddha famously advised that one should always try to be "not too tight and not too loose." It takes a certain flexibility of mind to navigate the various situations of our lives without falling into either of these extremes. The key ingredient in that flexibility is humor. Having a sense of humor implies that you're open to how things spontaneously occur. You don't have such fixed notions of how it all has to go and how you have to be. In fact, what's often most hilarious is when you're trying to make things go one way and they end up going in a totally wrong direction, like you're trying to paint your room beige and it turns out pink.

Trungpa Rinpoche would sometimes use humor as a means of helping us connect to our open awareness. At one of his teachings, he told a joke that everyone already knew from beginning to end. It was one of those jokes of the "pope and rabbi" variety. But Rinpoche managed to drag it out so that it lasted almost an hour and a half. It was so hilarious that we all wished he'd stop because of how much our ribs hurt from laughing. And then he stopped and just rested in open awareness. Everyone was so loosened up and relaxed that joining him in that basic spaciousness and clarity came naturally. When our mind is full of the warmth of humor, we are in touch with the best of ourselves.

19

Learning from Our Teachers

*Authentic teachers show us what it actually looks like
to go beyond fixed mind, to exist without polarizing, to
live joyfully in a state of groundlessness. They may still
have further to go on their own paths, but they have gone
far in letting go of their false samsaric comforts and in
overcoming their habitual patterns and reactions.*

AS WE ALL KNOW, BUT SOMETIMES FORGET, THE COM-
pany we keep is very important. In his *Thirty-Seven
Practices of a Bodhisattva*, Thogme Zangpo talks about this
point in two stanzas. The first is about avoiding negative influences: "With some friends, the poisons keep growing. Study,
reflection, and meditation weaken, while loving-kindness and
compassion fall away. Give up bad friends. This is the practice of a bodhisattva."

By "poisons" he means emotions such as anger and jealousy and obsessive desire. Being in the presence of certain
friends and situations churns up these emotions. For instance, if you're working to overcome an addiction to alcohol or drugs, being with people who like to indulge in those

substances increases the odds against you. Or if you want to stop having a negative view of people, you may have to abstain from hanging out with your friend the misanthrope. Or, as I mentioned in the previous chapter, if you have a friend you love to gossip with, you may have to come to a mutual agreement to stop.

"Bad friends" may bring to mind a monstrous image like Darth Vader, but the verse is just talking about how easy it is for us to get sidetracked, distracted, seduced. When we're with certain people or in certain situations, we lose our sense of what to do and what not to do. All the words of wisdom we've heard and understood lose their power to affect our mind. We forget about the preciousness of this life, in which we have access to so many teachings and so many methods for waking up. When we spend too much time with the wrong influences, we lose our ability to sit with raw, uncomfortable energy. We become more self-involved, narrow-minded, and negative. We have more and more trouble seeing our own basic goodness and that of others.

The next stanza of the *Thirty-Seven Practices* talks about a relationship that is intended to have the opposite effect. This is a relationship with a spiritual teacher or spiritual friend: "With some teachers, your shortcomings fade away and abilities grow like the waxing moon. Hold such teachers dear to you, dearer than your own body. This is the practice of a bodhisattva."

Some people naturally bring out the best in us. In their presence, we become more noble, brave, and altruistic. We become less cynical, petty, and self-doubting. Most of us probably know a number of people who have this kind of effect on us, and in the Buddhist lineage that I've been part of for many years, this role is exemplified by the spiritual teacher. I hold my teachers, beginning with Chögyam Trungpa Rinpoche, so dear to me because of how they've been able to show me—and model for me—my own potential. It's like meeting a part of yourself that you didn't even know was there.

Before I met Trungpa Rinpoche, I had no sense of how I habitually held on to fixed ideas, labels, and imputed meanings. I had no inkling of how I continually resisted what is, and how I could learn to relax that resistance and gradually begin to live in the free, open space of egolessness. I had no idea that my mind and heart had the potential to awaken, and to feel growing connectedness and concern for all living beings.

Authentic teachers show us what it actually looks like to go beyond fixed mind, to exist without polarizing, to live joyfully in a state of groundlessness. They may still have further to go on their own paths, but they have gone far in letting go of their false samsaric comforts and in overcoming their habitual patterns and reactions. They may still go through experiences such as anger or insecurity, but these emotions don't knock them off their seat. They're able to stay fully present, with an open, fresh, unbiased mind. When we are in their presence, we experience that open mind as well. We feel inspired to make the most of our life.

When you encounter the wide-openness of the teacher's mind, it resonates with the wide-openness of your own mind. You see how there is really no essential difference between your awareness and the teacher's awareness. And you see that you can accomplish what they've accomplished because all of us have had to start in the same place—as confused, reactive, but basically good human beings. Through instruction and by example, the teacher shows us it's possible.

The Vajrayana tradition, to which Trungpa Rinpoche and my other main teachers belong, places an especially strong emphasis on the teacher-student relationship. As a result, there can be a feeling of mystique around a teacher, which sometimes leads to people looking for a teacher almost desperately. "Is this my teacher? Is this my teacher? This one looks really good. I like this person's teachings. They really make sense to me. So, this person *must* be my teacher."

What I've found, in the Vajrayana at least, is that the most important thing in finding a teacher is your heart connection. It's comparable to falling in love. Some people who are looking for love make a list of requirements and then go looking for a partner who fits those requirements. But finding someone who looks good on paper doesn't usually lead to falling deeply in love. Similarly, while there are certainly requirements for spiritual teachers—for instance, that they understand the teachings deeply and always have your best interests in mind—you need to do more than check off a list to discover a deep heart connection.

Just as people fall in love in many different ways, there are many different ways of meeting and forming a bond with a spiritual teacher. The story of how I formed a relationship with Trungpa Rinpoche shows how there's no formula for how this should go. I personally resonated with Rinpoche, but what I felt in his presence didn't exactly correspond to what I thought I was supposed to feel with "my teacher." Some texts talk about your hair standing on end and tears streaming down your face. That didn't happen with me. Part of it was that I found him so intimidating. I often wondered to myself if he was really the teacher for me.

At one point, Trungpa Rinpoche brought His Holiness the

Sixteenth Karmapa to the United States. I saw His Holiness sitting on the throne—a big man in brocade clothing, gorgeous and awe-inspiring. I had the tears down my cheeks, the on-fire feeling, the whole shebang. Then I requested an interview with him. His presence was profound, but when I asked him a typically Western question, he said something out of a traditional text that I didn't understand. Trungpa Rinpoche, on the other hand, was very skillful in working with my Western mind. He saw who I was and where I was stuck, and he had an incredible way of getting to the heart of the matter and cutting through my neuroses with his answers. I thought, "Now what? One can answer my questions, but I don't get the tears coming down my cheeks. With the other one, I have the tears, but I don't understand his answers. What am I supposed to do?"

Since I was living in Boulder, Colorado, where Trungpa Rinpoche also lived, it was natural for me to be part of his sangha and to do the practices he gave us. But since I still felt hesitation about fully committing to be his student I decided to get to know him better. Different students have different needs, but for me it was important to be able to see what my teacher was like not only on a stage in front of an audience, but at a more ordinary, day-to-day level.

I had to search for a way to make this happen, and eventually I was given the responsibility of taking care of his shrines. He had a shrine in the sitting room off his bedroom and another one downstairs, and he personally showed me how to care for them. I still found him as terrifying and intimidating when I saw him eating breakfast as I did when he was teaching, but I also saw things about him that made me fall in love with him and trust him completely. I saw how he would try anything to wake people up and how he never gave up on anyone. I saw how he was totally committed to everyone's enlightenment—that was all he cared about. I saw how selflessly he loved his students. By observing all this, I finally overcame all my doubts and hesitations. So that's the story of my personal journey to making a heart connection with my teacher.

Thogme Zangpo's verse says that "your shortcomings fade away," but in my experience, when you work with a teacher, your shortcomings appear to become heightened. It's as if you've always had pimples all over your face but you never noticed because you didn't have a mirror. It's not that my teachers meant to be critical of me, but their mirror-like effect made everything become so clear. And because you admire your teacher, you want to come off looking especially good in front of them, so you wish you had fewer pimples in their presence. But after a while, you realize that trying to look good isn't working, and you just give it up. You come as you are. And you realize that's what the teacher has been encouraging you to do all along: don't hide anything and come as you are.

Spiritual teachers have to earn your trust. All the traditional teachings recommend examining them carefully and determining to the best of your ability that their only motivation is to help you wake up. But once that happens, they can only help you if you trust them. Then they can do wondrous things, such as leading you directly into an experience of emptiness. In the Vajrayana, the teacher gives "pointing out instructions," which introduce the experience of "mind itself," the mind of open awareness that each of us already has but can't usually recognize. This can be a similar experience to what happens when a room full of people slap their thighs at the same time, but it is especially powerful in the presence of the teacher. Teachers use different ways of stopping your mind so that you experience an extended gap in your thinking and labeling process. In that space, a lot of insight comes about the true nature of things and you can see how locked up you usually are in the habitual patterns of your mind.

For me, when I'm with my teachers, I can feel my own open awareness simply by being in their presence. It can even come when I think about them or picture their faces. Because they dwell in that vast, empty space beyond thoughts and labels, when I am open to them, it's possible to be in that space with them. I am welcome to join them in that sacred, compassionate atmosphere, which is neither theirs nor mine.

I remember once waiting to have an interview with Trungpa Rinpoche. I was sitting outside his room in tears, completely worked up. But when I went in and sat down in front of him, I entered that limitless space of awareness that he always inhabited. It was so sudden that I found myself trying desperately to bring the tears back, so I could convince him how terrible everything was. Finally, when I managed to get myself worked up again, he yawned and looked out the window! This was really painful, but it totally stopped my mind. All my propensities were up strong, but with all that space, they had nowhere to get stuck. It was just as Trungpa Rinpoche used to say, "When your mind is big, thoughts are like mosquitoes buzzing around with nowhere to land."

In many situations, however, there is no way to get close to a teacher as I did with Trungpa Rinpoche. The teacher may live far away or have so many students that he or she doesn't know their individual peculiarities—or even their names. People often wonder if these circumstances make it impossible for them to benefit from this kind of teacher-student relationship. Are they too far from the teacher's fire to receive any warmth?

My feeling is, whatever amount of contact you do have with an authentic teacher, if you take to heart what he or she is teaching you, then that can be enough to turn your whole life into a path of awakening. If what the teacher says really rings true for you, then you will start to find opportunities to practice everywhere. I spill ink down the front of my favorite coat—opportunity to practice. The actions of other students drive me crazy and I'm full of criticisms and dislike—opportunity to practice.

A friend of mine has an intense phobia of being in confined spaces. Not knowing this, a fellow student asked her to help clean out the retreat center's water cistern. This involved climbing down into a small dark space and cleaning off the slimy, sticky cistern's walls. Naturally, she said, "No way," and explained her phobia. But within half an hour, this brave woman decided she wanted to face her fears rather than run from them and she agreed to join two other students in that dark, confined space. It wasn't comfortable, but she worked through some of her oldest fears. Since then, whenever fears arise, she refers to that as "a chance for cistern practice," a chance to take the teachings to heart and apply them.

Every challenge presents an opportunity for spiritual growth, whether it's a small irritation or when everything as you've known it falls apart. Perhaps the ultimate challenge for any student comes if they find out that their teacher has betrayed their trust. This happens far too often in spiritual communities. Seemingly out of nowhere, the all-too-human aspect of the teacher is uncovered in all its unpleasant details.

You were just beginning to warm up to this teacher, or you had already developed a deep love and respect for him or her, and suddenly your world is turned upside down. As it is commonly said, the "shadow side" of our teacher has been revealed.

What then? Do you cling to "he or she can do no wrong"? Or do you go to the other extreme and reject them completely? The decision about whether to leave the spiritual community and the teacher is a really hard one and very personal. But the decision about whether to close your heart and mind or to stay open and vulnerable is to me the most important thing. Many have left their teachers because of behavior they couldn't condone, yet at the same time always remembered the teacher's kindness and always continued to appreciate what the teacher had taught them.

How to keep an un-fixated mind and a tender heart in times like this becomes a student's koan. You might find that this becomes the greatest teaching of your life, or you might find that it is time for you to leave. In either case, how to keep your mind clear enough to see that harm has been done, yet open enough to allow for a person—any person—to learn from their mistakes and evolve—this is the challenge. We usually want clear-cut results and right or wrong conclusions. But when we let life unfold free of our value judgments, it can take very surprising and unexpected twists and turns, and it will always teach us a lot.

But is it even possible to hold "I do not condone this behavior," or "I feel angry and betrayed," with "I love and care for this person"? This is an important question. It's similar to when a close friend or beloved family member messes up in a major way. Sometimes we turn against them and won't have anything further to do with them. A surprising number of people, however, somehow find a way to not condone or enable but, at the same time, not withdraw their love. I remember Trungpa Rinpoche saying that no matter what a person has done, you should always keep the door open. This is hard practice for sure. It requires stepping out of the comfort zone big-time. It requires developing the capacity to experience the deep learning and growth of the challenge zone and be transformed by it.

It isn't easy for anyone to embrace a koan of this magnitude, and it wouldn't surprise me to learn that for you this simply isn't an option, at least not right now. What then? I've found that the sanest way forward is to simply acknowledge where you are without guilt or arrogance, make whatever decision you need to make, and move on with your life. But while moving on, you can also aspire to not let this experience narrow your mind or harden your heart. You can aspire that it deepen your commitment to self-reflection and tenderness. Then wherever you go your learning will continue. Your journey to enlightenment will continue.

The teacher helps you wake up by mirroring both your shortcomings and your basic goodness. He or she shows you both the neuroses you didn't want to look at and the potential that you didn't know was there. But once you've started getting familiar with these aspects of your mind and have acquired a taste to see more and more, the whole world opens up to you as your teacher. This is called "finding the universal teacher," the teacher as the phenomenal world.

20

Mission Impossible

Instead of seeing it as futile or depressing, we can see the limitlessness of the job ahead of us as a source of continual inspiration.

WHEN I GIVE PUBLIC TALKS, I SOMETIMES LIKE to begin by asking everyone to recite with me the following traditional lines:

> May bodhichitta, precious and sublime,
> Arise where it has not yet come to be;
> And where it has arisen, may it never fail,
> But grow and flourish ever more and more.

These lines summarize the entire bodhisattva path, the journey we undertake to awaken our hearts and minds so that we can be of greater and greater benefit to others.

The first two lines refer to the time before we've been introduced to the idea of bodhichitta, the aspiration and commitment to wake up for the benefit of others. However, no one is really starting from scratch. Bodhichitta is based on love and compassion, which we all have in our hearts.

Some people, especially when they've had traumatic or very difficult relationships with family members, have the idea that they don't really love anyone. But there's always somebody—if not a person, then at least a cat or a dog. We all have at least a glimmer of bodhichitta. As Trungpa Rinpoche liked to say, "Everyone loves something, even if it's only tortillas."

The third line encourages us to value whatever glimmer of bodhichitta we have, to protect and take care of it so that it doesn't diminish. It's like when you see the first flowers coming up in the spring—you feel a soft spot for them and want them to do well, so you avoid stepping on them and try to keep animals from chewing them. In the case of bodhichitta at this early stage, we have to protect it from our own habits, such as tendencies to polarize or to focus too much on ourselves at the expense of others.

In addition to protecting our bodhichitta, we have to do whatever we can to help it grow. This doesn't just happen on its own; it takes effort. It's said that we should grasp bodhichitta as a blind person in a desert would grasp the tail of a cow. Imagine you're blind, lost in the desert, and desperately thirsty. If you heard a cow walking by, you'd realize it could lead you to water, so the smart thing would be to grasp its tail and make sure never to let go. This analogy also gives us a sense of how important bodhichitta is. If you're dying of thirst, you probably won't be thinking, "It would be kind of nice to get a glass of water. Instead, all your thoughts would be about how to find water. You would think of anyone or anything you encountered—even a cow—as a potential way of getting water.

In a similar way, as we get acquainted with our own broken

heart and gradually discover that the vulnerability, discomfort, and confusion we feel is the same vulnerability, discomfort, and confusion that everyone experiences, we develop a powerful longing to awaken rather than stay asleep. Eventually, waking up in order to help others becomes the main concern of our life. When we become fully preoccupied with bodhichitta in this way, we become resourceful in using every situation of our life to wake up.

At first, it takes a lot of effort to keep going forward on the path of awakening. A big part of that effort is noticing when you're triggered or worked up and then doing something different from your usual reaction. That reaction might be to act out physically or verbally, or to immerse yourself in a convincing storyline about what that person did, or how inferior I am, or how terrible everything is, or how much better things would be if only (fill in the blank).

Instead of reacting in any of these habitual ways, you may have to do things that seem a little artificial. For instance, someone may look at you in a certain way that brings up a chronic self-image you have of being wounded, or "damaged goods." At that point, instead of becoming angry or despondent, you could go against your habit and think to yourself, "May I and all the other people in the world who feel this inadequacy be free of it." You can make the thought even bigger: "May this difficult encounter somehow be the seed for my awakening, and for the awakening of everyone who feels inadequate, and for everyone else's awakening as well." This may feel a little phony, but it's similar to building a muscle that you haven't used much before. It's like running. If you have the longing and commitment to get fit, then at first, you might have to make an awkward effort to put on your shoes and hit the trail. You have to go even when you really don't want to go. But eventually, without your even noticing how it changed, running becomes natural. You find that your desire to run is much greater than your desire not to.

As you build up your bodhichitta muscles, your attitude about adversity changes. Whenever something unpleasant or unwelcome happens, you may still not like it, but you see it as an opportunity to shift something in your own mind and heart. This shift changes your life. But it's not like a single event that happens at a particular time, like Monday at noon. It's a transformation that gradually creeps up on you.

Shantideva compares bodhichitta to a wish-fulfilling tree that never stops bearing fruit, as opposed to a plantain tree that produces fruit just once and then dies. The plantain tree is like an ordinary good deed. Your friend has a headache and you give her an aspirin. You do a kind thing, which has a good result, but that's the end of it. Your intention is limited to doing one act for one person at one time. With bodhichitta, on the other hand, everything you do becomes part of a much vaster intention. You still give your friend the aspirin, but that kind deed is part of a much greater wish that your friend eventually wake up from suffering and confusion altogether. And that wish is part of a still greater one—to help all sentient beings, without a single exception, to wake up completely.

The ultimate wish of bodhichitta is so vast and all-inclusive that it's sometimes referred to as "mission impossible." First of all, in order to make this wish, we have to come to terms with the no-exceptions clause. It's easy to come up with a list of people who *must* be exceptions, such as ruthless dictators, people who delight in being cruel to animals, or anyone who's done terrible things to you or your loved ones. These so-called "evil people" seem to enjoy the suffering of others. But imagine if Adolf Hitler had woken up fully and become free from suffering. Would he have done any of the things he did? Would anyone purposely harm others if they were able to hold the rawness of vulnerability in their heart instead of reacting ignorantly from their emotional pain? When we ask ourselves these questions, we see how much sense it makes not to have any exceptions to our bodhichitta aspirations.

We can also get overwhelmed or discouraged when we think about the limitless number of people and animals who are in desperate need of help. When we compare that to what we can actually do to relieve suffering, it may seem almost pointless to try. We talk about attaining enlightenment in order to free all beings from suffering, but could there really be an end to suffering?

Roshi Bernie Glassman, who spent decades working with homeless people in Yonkers, New York, said "I don't really believe there's going to be an end to homelessness, but I go in every day as if it's possible. And then I work individual by individual." That was also Mother Teresa's approach. She knew she couldn't end all the poverty in Calcutta. But she realized she could help many dying people feel loved, so she and her people worked on that every day, and her organization grew and grew.

The impossible mission of bodhichitta is like unrequited love. It's like the story of Romeo and Juliet, who couldn't get together, but whose love kept growing despite the fact that it could never be satisfied. The longing to help all beings wake up can draw us out of ourselves, out and out until we enter the realm of vast mind and vast heart. Eventually, we will realize the full potential of our mind is so much vaster than what our present low-tech sense perceptions can see. And what we can do for others—even though it's not everything—is equally vast. Instead of seeing it as futile or depressing, we can see the limitlessness of the job ahead of us as a source of continual inspiration—an endless opportunity for our precious bodhichitta to "grow and flourish ever more and more."

These days, many of us feel anxiety and gloom when we look around or read the news. This is natural and understandable, but at the same time it's important to find ways of cultivating optimism. As it says in an aspiration that I recite often, "In relating to the future of humanity, I will be optimistic and courageous." Without having some sense of optimism, it's easy to fall into a passive or defeatist attitude. Why try to do anything to improve the future if it's hopeless anyway? But according to the teachings on karma, the future is unwritten. What we do now does matter, not just to ourselves but to everyone who is part of this web of interconnection that we call Mother Earth. Even smiling at someone once can have a tremendous ripple effect that goes out and out—who knows how far? If this is the case, then think of how much we can affect the world by enthusiastically training in opening our hearts and minds, day after day.

But while being optimistic, it's also important to be realistic. Although many people engage in a continual stream of positive actions, many others act habitually out of confusion, fear, and self-interest. Some are planting mostly positive seeds for the future, some mostly negative, and the majority are planting both. We don't really know what all this will add up to. If our idea of being optimistic is to think and speak in a naively positive way about what the future will bring, that may lead to a lot of discouragement when we see how things actually unfold.

In South Africa, people who had suffered under apartheid were incredibly inspired when Nelson Mandela became president and then when the Truth and Reconciliation Commission came together. But many of those who thought things would continue in this spirit became cynical as the pace of transformation slowed down and corruption and suffering increased. A lot of people working to help others in South Africa and other places have crashed and burned upon seeing progress slow down or even reverse. On the other hand, there are still many people in these roles who continue to feel inspired and keep working courageously, whatever the immediate results.

Trungpa Rinpoche had a strong intuitive sense of the future, and what he saw wasn't pretty—natural disasters, economic crises, and increasing physical and mental discomfort. He saw that this could either bring out the worst in people or the best in people. Some, because of their legitimate fear of not having enough, or losing whatever they had, would get mean and selfish. But there would also be those who could rise to the occasion and help others make it through adversity. He said it was up to us to decide which way we wanted to meet the future.

We can begin to prepare for the future by asking ourselves a few questions. What will I do and how will I be when unwanted events occur? Will I be able to maintain a steady mind and a kind heart that can accommodate whatever pain arises and therefore benefit myself and society rather than be a hindrance? How will I react to illness, to devastating loss, to insults and disrespect? What about when things get worse in the environment or in politics? Will I freak out and erupt in hatred, fear, or self-condemnation? Or will my practice allow me to be with what I'm feeling and proceed sanely and humanely? Will adversity bring out my basest qualities or will it bring out my best ones?

Having asked ourselves these kinds of questions, we can then start using what comes up in our present lives to prepare for the future. From this point on, we can train in staying open and compassionate in whatever difficult circumstances we encounter. Then, if we get to a point where hardships bring out the best in us, we will be of great help to those in whom hardships bring out the worst. If even a small number of people become peaceful warriors in this way, that group will be able to help many others just by their example.

Dzigar Kongtrul Rinpoche is an advocate of this kind of courageous and practical realism. He urges people to train in becoming "modern-day bodhisattvas," or simply "MDBs." His students have even designed an MDB baseball cap to inspire themselves and others to move through the world with an altruistic, resilient heart. This work is based on getting to know how things really are and conducting ourselves bravely and creatively within that framework.

His Holiness the Dalai Lama says, "When the old pretend to be young and the foolish pretend to be intelligent, it is better to just be realistic." His Holiness has worked to develop programs to bring compassion and empathy into the education of children all over the world. He sees how almost all the suffering and chaos in the world is caused by the mentality of "us and them." This is what's behind all the "isms" that bring about much of today's rampant violence, callousness, and self-righteousness. "Compassion is not at all religious business," he says. "It is important to know it is human business. It is a question of human survival." In other words, there's more at stake in learning about spirituality and meditation than just trying to feel good about yourself or getting better at relaxing. Replacing "us and them" with a feeling of our universal sameness and interconnectedness is becoming a practical requirement for survival.

We can be realistic and optimistic at the same time because, ultimately, the view of the Dharma is encouraging and life-affirming. The Buddha taught that all beings have the potential to wake up completely, and that all of us will eventually get there. He and many other wise people in this world have given us tools for taking whatever occurs in our lives and using it to cultivate our basic goodness and become more and more able to be there for others. Whatever the future brings—welcome or unwelcome—we can use on our path of awakening. To me, this attitude is the best kind of optimism. As we keep opening up to our potential as bodhisattvas, we will go from having a tiny view of ourselves and our world to discovering a boundless capacity to care for and benefit our fellow living beings.

PRACTICES FOR WELCOMING THE UNWELCOME

Basic Sitting Meditation

THE TECHNIQUE OF SITTING MEDITATION CALLED *shamatha-vipashyana* ("tranquility-insight") is like a golden key that helps us to know ourselves. In shamatha-vipashyana meditation, we sit upright with legs crossed and eyes open, hands resting on our thighs. Then we simply become aware of our breath as it goes out. It requires precision to be right there with that breath. On the other hand, it's extremely relaxed and extremely soft. Saying, "Be right there with the breath as it goes out," is the same thing as saying, "Be fully present." Be right here with whatever is going on. Being aware of the breath as it goes out, we may also be aware of other things going on—sounds on the street, the light on the walls. These things may capture our attention slightly, but they don't need to draw us off. We can continue to sit right here, aware of the breath going out.

The text of "Basic Sitting Meditation" originally appeared in *Start Where You Are: A Guide to Compassionate Living,* © 1994 by Pema Chödrön.

But being with the breath is only part of the technique. These thoughts that run through our minds continually are the other part. We sit here talking to ourselves. The instruction is that when you realize you've been thinking, you label it "thinking." When your mind wanders off, you say to yourself, "Thinking." Whether your thoughts are violent or passionate or full of ignorance and denial; whether your thoughts are worried or fearful; whether your thoughts are spiritual thoughts, pleasing thoughts of how well you're doing, comforting thoughts, uplifting thoughts—whatever they are, without judgment or harshness simply label it all "thinking," and do that with honesty and gentleness.

The touch on the breath is light: only about 25 percent of the awareness is on the breath. You're not grasping or fixating on it. You're opening, letting the breath mix with the space of the room, letting your breath just go out into space. Then there's something like a pause, a gap until the next breath goes out again. While you're breathing in, there could be some sense of just opening and waiting. It is like pushing the doorbell and waiting for someone to answer. Then you push the doorbell again and wait for someone to answer. Then probably your mind wanders off and you realize you're thinking again—at this point, use the labeling technique.

It's important to be faithful to the technique. If you find that your labeling has a harsh, negative tone to it, as if you were saying, "Dammit!," that you're giving yourself a hard time, say "thinking" again and lighten up. It's not like trying to down the thoughts as if they were clay pigeons. Instead, be gentle. Use the labeling part of the technique as an opportunity to develop softness and compassion for yourself.

Anything that comes up is okay in the arena of meditation. The point is, you can see it honestly and make friends with it.

Although it is embarrassing and painful, it is very healing to stop hiding from yourself. It is healing to know all the ways that you're sneaky, all the ways that you hide out, criticize people, all the ways that you shut down, deny, close off, all your weird little ways. You can know all that with some sense of humor and kindness. By knowing yourself, you're coming to know humanness altogether. We are all up against these things. We are all in this together. When you realize that you're talking to yourself, label it "thinking" and notice your tone of voice. Let it be compassionate and gentle and humorous. Then you'll be changing old stuck patterns that are shared by the whole human race. Compassion for others begins with kindness to ourselves.

Tonglen Practice

TONGLEN PRACTICE IS A METHOD FOR CONNECTING with suffering—our own and that which is all around us, everywhere we go. It is a method for overcoming our fear of suffering and for dissolving the tightness of our hearts. Primarily it is a method for awakening the compassion that is inherent in all of us, no matter how cruel or cold we might seem to be.

We begin the practice by taking on the suffering of a person whom we know to be hurting and wish to help. For instance, if we know of a child who is being hurt, we breathe in with the wish to take away all of that child's pain and fear. Then, as we breathe out, we send happiness, joy, or whatever would relieve the child. This is the core of the practice: breathing in others' pain so they can be well and have more space to relax and open—breathing out, sending them

The text of "Tonglen Practice" is adapted from *When Things Fall Apart: Heart Advice for Difficult Times,* © 1997 by Pema Chödrön.

relaxation or whatever we feel would bring them relief and happiness.

Often, however, we can't do this practice because we come face to face with our own fear, our own resistance or anger, or whatever personal pain we have just then.

At that point we can change the focus and begin to do tonglen for what we are feeling and for millions of other people just like us who at that very moment are feeling exactly the same stuckness and misery. Maybe we are able to name our pain. We recognize it clearly as terror or revulsion or anger or wanting to get revenge. We breathe in for all the people who are caught with that same emotion, and we send our relief or whatever opens up the space for ourselves and all those countless others. Maybe we can't name what we're feeling. But we can feel it—a tightness in the stomach, a heavy darkness, or whatever. We simply contact what we are feeling and breathe in, take it *in*, for all of us—and send *out* relief to all of us.

People often say that this practice goes against the grain of how we usually hold ourselves together. Truthfully, this practice *does* go against the grain of wanting things on our own terms, wanting everything to work out for ourselves no matter what happens to the others. The practice dissolves the walls we've built around our hearts. It dissolves the layers of self-protection we've tried so hard to create. In Buddhist language, one would say that it dissolves the fixation and clinging of ego.

Tonglen reverses the usual logic of avoiding suffering and seeking pleasure. In the process, we become liberated from very ancient patterns of selfishness. We begin to feel love for both ourselves and others; we begin to take care of ourselves and others. Tonglen awakens our compassion and introduces us to a far bigger view of reality. At first this allows us to experience things as not such a big deal and not so solid as they seemed before. We start to connect with the open dimension of our being. With practice, we become familiar with the unlimited spaciousness of *shunyata*.

Tonglen can be done for those who are ill, those who are dying or have died, those who are in pain of any kind. It can be done as a formal meditation practice or right on the spot at any time. We are out walking and we see someone in pain—right on the spot we can begin to breathe in that person's pain and send out relief. Or we are just as likely to see someone in pain and look away. The pain brings up our fear or anger; it brings up our resistance and confusion. So, on the spot we can do tonglen for all the people just like ourselves, all those who wish to be compassionate but instead are afraid—who wish to be brave but instead are cowardly. Rather than beating ourselves up, we can use our personal stuckness as a stepping-stone to understanding what people are up against all over the world. Breathe in for all of us and breathe out for all of us. Use what seems like poison as medicine. We can use our personal suffering as the path to compassion for all beings.

When you do tonglen on the spot, simply breathe in and breathe out, taking in pain and sending out spaciousness and relief.

When you do tonglen as a formal meditation practice, it has four stages:

First, rest your mind briefly, for a second or two, in a state of openness or stillness. This stage is traditionally called "flashing on absolute bodhichitta," or suddenly opening to basic spaciousness and clarity. What that means is a moment free of fixed mind—a completely open, fresh moment before thinking and bias set in.

If you have trouble connecting to this openness, you can bring to mind an image of a wide-open experience from your life. You can think about standing on the beach and looking out at the vast ocean or being high up in the mountains under an immense sky, with an expansive view of many miles. Or you can ring a gong and listen to its sound as a way of touching in with that fresh, still mind, free of fixation. Whatever you need to do, the point is to connect to a place of open mind and open heart, which is the background for the rest of the practice.

Second, work with texture. When you inhale, breathe in a feeling of hot, dark, and heavy. This is the claustrophobic texture and quality of tightly fixed mind. Visualize or somehow have the experience of taking in this discomfort. Breathe it in completely, through all the pores of your body. For some people, it's helpful to think in terms of colors or images. A traditional image is breathing in black smoke. Some breathe in red because it's hot; some visualize green slimy stuff. You can do whatever works to give you the sense of taking in these uncomfortable feelings that you would normally avoid.

When you exhale, breathe out a feeling of cool, bright, airy, and light—a sense of freshness. Again, you can use whatever imagery works, such as the coolness of blue, or the brightness of white. Radiate this freshness 360 degrees, through all the pores of your body. Let it be a very complete experience. Continue for a while breathing these textures in and out. Keep going until they feel synchronized with your breath.

In the third stage, connect with a personal situation that's painful to you. For instance, if your elderly mother is going through a hard time, breathe in her pain with the wish that she be free of any pain she's having. With your out-breath send out happiness or spaciousness or whatever you think will benefit her. Or you can think about an animal that you know is in a cruel, abusive situation. On the in-breath, take in the pain of their experience, and on the out-breath imagine the animal free and happy.

For this stage, you can use anything that naturally moves you, anything that feels personal and real. However, as I described, if you are stuck, you can do the practice for the pain you are feeling and simultaneously for all those just like you who feel that kind of suffering. For instance, if you are feeling inadequate, you breathe that in for yourself and all the others in the same boat, and you send out confidence and adequacy or relief in any form you wish.

Finally, in the fourth stage, we expand on the specific situation and make our taking in and sending out bigger. The third and fourth stages balance each other out. The idea is that if you're too general, it doesn't really touch the heart. But if you stay too specific, you can get bogged down, overwhelmed, or too self-absorbed about the particular situation.

If you started out by doing tonglen for your mother, then extend that to all people who are in her situation, or to all elderly people in general. If you are thinking about an abused animal, expand that to all abused animals, or all animals in any form of pain. But if these contemplations start to feel too general or abstract, come back to the specific case that is more personal to you.

If you began with your own experience of suffering, such as your feeling of inadequacy, expand that contemplation. Do tonglen for those close to you who feel inadequate and then go wider and wider, universalizing that feeling. When you start getting too distant, come back to your own inadequacy. Taste it, smell it, really experience it—and then go back to universalizing.

Another way to go from stages three to four is to expand out from those whom you easily care about to those who are further and further from the center of your care. After doing tonglen for someone close to you, try doing it for a stranger, someone you know nothing about and who doesn't arouse any strong positive or negative feelings for you. Breathe in with the aspiration that they be free of any pain they may have. Breathe in with the wish that they be free from fixed mind. Then breathe out feelings of peace and joy, especially the spaciousness and stillness of their fundamentally open mind and heart.

From there, try to expand your heart beyond what currently seems possible. Think of someone you find difficult. Don't go with your scariest person right away—perhaps just think of someone who irritates you. Call to mind their face or their name—anything that brings them near. Then do tonglen for them. And as your capacity increases, try doing tonglen for those people who challenge you the most.

Finally, expand your tonglen more and more throughout space. Do it for everyone in your local area, then in wider and wider circles until your taking and sending covers the whole globe. Do it for all the women in the world who are hurting. Do it for all the men, all the children, all the animals. See if you can really stretch and do tonglen for the whole planet— for all the water, the air, and the land, which are all hurting. Do it as if you were on the moon looking back at the earth. Do tonglen for the whole planet and all the beings on the planet—wishing that all living beings could go beyond the fixated mind of "us and them," that we could all regard ourselves as one family and live together in a state of complete peace and harmony. Ultimately, you can do tonglen for all beings, wherever they may be throughout the universe.

Tonglen can extend infinitely. As you do the practice, gradually over time your compassion naturally expands, and so does your realization that things are not as solid as you thought. As you do this practice, gradually at your own pace, you will be surprised to find yourself more and more able to be there for others even in what used to seem like impossible situations.

Locate, Embrace, Stop, Remain

L.E.S.R.—PRONOUNCED LIKE "LASER"—STANDS FOR "locate, embrace, stop, remain" and is a practice developed by Richard Reoch, a well-known human rights worker and a former president of Shambhala International. You can use it as a concise and easy-to-remember way of combining some of the practices in this book for welcoming the unwelcome.

Whenever you feel yourself getting worked up or having any unpleasant, uncomfortable, or stuck feelings, follow these four steps.

1. **LOCATE** it. Investigate where that grasping, contracted sensation dwells in your body, and make contact with it.
2. **EMBRACE** that feeling, that sensation, that contraction. One way of doing this is by following Tsoknyi Rinpoche's instruction to send any fearful, grasping, self-protective feelings your unconditional warmth. This can be similar to calming a hysterical child. The main point is to reverse the ancient human tendency

to avoid and reject pain. Instead you move toward it with heart.

3. **STOP** the storyline. "Stop" works for the acronym, but I think of this step more as letting go of, interrupting, or looking directly at the thoughts and stories. The idea is not to stop thinking altogether, which isn't possible, but to go beneath or behind your thoughts to contact the underlying sense of being hooked. You can learn a lot just by having a direct, nonconceptual experience of being hooked, even if it only lasts for a moment. Once you've connected with that raw feeling, you can then continue to interrupt the stories and keep returning to the experience again and again. Having a regular meditation practice will help you tremendously with this step.

4. **REMAIN.** Stay present with the feeling. Keep going until it shifts, or until it feels like too much of a struggle. You don't have to wait until you feel overwhelmed. This is not an endurance trial. Just remain with the feeling with kindness and warmth, leaning in as much as you can. What often happens at this time is you discover how painful the feeling is and realize you don't want to continue to do that to yourself. This can soften you up considerably and can also make you more accessible to see and hear other people. It can give your natural intelligence and openness a chance to emerge.

Once you've worked with these four steps for a while, you can try adding a fifth step. Here there are two main alternatives.

The first is what I call "experiencing the emptiness of the feeling." There are various ways to experiment with this, but they all have to do with the insight—however fleeting—that one's suffering comes not from the feeling per se, but from the sense of there being a suffer*er*.

For example, while you are staying present with the feeling beneath the storyline, ask yourself, "Who is feeling this?" Pause and contemplate. Then ask the question again: "Who is feeling this?" You can repeat this process a few times if you find it helpful.

You can also come at experiencing the emptiness of the feeling from other angles. You can explore questions such as: "Is this feeling permanent?" "Is it transient?" "Is it solid?" "Is it fluid?" "Is it fixed?" "Is it dynamic?" "Is it finite or infinite?" You can also ask: "Is this feeling me?" "Is it not me?" "Is it an obstacle?" "Is it a portal?" Or you can touch the feeling, completely free of storyline, and say, "When experienced directly, this very feeling is basic goodness," or "Basic goodness is found right here." In other words, you don't have to wait until the feeling is gone to find basic goodness.

An alternative fifth step is to experiment with using the feeling as a way to awaken compassion. While remaining present with the raw feeling, contemplate that countless people and animals all over the planet are feeling just like this. Use your experience as a way of gaining insight into our sameness with one another. At this point, you can contemplate along these lines: "May I and all beings who feel like this be free from our pain. May we be free from the underlying contraction and fear that come from defending our personal territory." You can also take this opportunity to practice tonglen, breathing in and deeply opening to the shared feeling, and then breathing out relief to all beings (including your fearful, contracted self) who are caught in the same way.

Both of these fifth steps are based on the same idea. Tapping into your innate capacity to experience your feelings directly and nonconceptually gives you a doorway to going deeper into experiencing emptiness and compassion. At first, emptiness and compassion seem like separate things, but eventually you will experience them in their basic essence as inseparable and nondual.

L.E.S.R. and its related practices provide you with the means to expand your view and open your heart and mind at the very point where we all habitually contract and go inward. These are practices for a lifetime that you can begin today.

ACKNOWLEDGMENTS

I AM GRATEFUL to so many people who have made this book possible and I would like to thank a few of them by name. Megan Jacoby transcribed hours upon hours of my teachings, which made up the source material for this book. Barbara Abrams reviewed every chapter and contributed many valuable ideas. Rachel Neumann of Shambhala Publications asked important questions and found ways to clarify and fine-tune the final manuscript. Tami Simon generously gave permission to use material from my 2014 Naropa University graduation speech, which was first published by Sounds True as "Fail, Fail Again, Fail Better." Mark Wilding of PassageWorks introduced me to the phrase that became the title for this book as well as to the three concentric circles in the comfort zone chapter. My friend Ken McLeod wrote *Reflections on Silver River*, a book that has deepened my understanding of the bodhisattva path considerably. And Joseph Waxman, who it is always a pleasure to work with, organized these teachings into chapters, paragraphs, and sentences; without him this book wouldn't exist.

Photograph by Christine Alicino

ABOUT THE AUTHOR

ANI PEMA CHÖDRÖN was born Deirdre Blomfield-Brown in 1936, in New York City. She attended Miss Porter's School in Connecticut and graduated from the University of California at Berkeley. She taught as an elementary school teacher for many years in both New Mexico and California. Pema has two children and three grandchildren.

While in her mid-thirties, Ani Pema traveled to the French Alps and encountered Lama Chime Rinpoche, with whom she studied for several years. She became a novice nun in 1974 while studying with Lama Chime in London. His Holiness the Sixteenth Karmapa came to Scotland at that time, and Ani Pema received her ordination from him.

Ani Pema first met her root guru, Chögyam Trungpa Rinpoche, in 1972. Lama Chime encouraged her to work with Rinpoche, and it was with him that she ultimately made her most profound connection, studying with him from 1974 until his death in 1987. At the request of the Sixteenth Karmapa, she received the full bhikshuni ordination in the Chinese lineage of Buddhism in 1981 in Hong Kong. She served as the director of Karma Dzong in Boulder, Colorado, until moving in 1984 to rural Cape Breton, Nova Scotia, to be the director of Gampo Abbey.

Chögyam Trungpa Rinpoche gave her explicit instructions on establishing this monastery for Western monks and nuns.

Ani Pema currently teaches in the United States and Canada and plans for an increased amount of time in solitary retreat under the guidance of Venerable Dzigar Kongtrul Rinpoche. She is interested in helping to establish Tibetan Buddhist monasticism in the West, as well as continuing her work with Western Buddhists of all traditions, sharing ideas and teachings. Her nonprofit, the Pema Chödrön Foundation, was set up to assist in this purpose.

She has written several books, including *The Wisdom of No Escape, Start Where You Are, When Things Fall Apart, The Places That Scare You, Becoming Bodhisattvas, Practicing Peace,* and *Living Beautifully.*

BOOKS AND AUDIO BY
PEMA CHÖDRÖN

BOOKS

Awakening Loving-Kindness

We often look far and wide for guidance to become better people, as though the answers were *somewhere out there*. But Pema Chödrön suggests that the best and most direct teacher for awakening loving-kindness is in fact *your very own life*. Based on talks given during a one-month meditation retreat at Gampo Abbey, where Pema lives and teaches, her teachings here focus on learning how to see the events of our lives as the perfect material for learning to love ourselves and our world playfully and wholeheartedly—and to live in our skin fearlessly, without aggression, harshness, or shame.

Becoming Bodhisattvas: A Guidebook for Compassionate Action

The Way of the Bodhisattva has long been treasured as an indispensable guide to enlightened living, offering a window into the greatest potential within us all. Written in the eighth century by the scholar and saint Shantideva, it presents a comprehensive view of the Mahayana Buddhist tradition's highest ideal—to commit oneself to the life of a bodhisattva warrior, a person who is wholeheartedly dedicated to the freedom and common good of all beings. In this comprehensive commentary, Pema Chödrön invites you to journey more deeply into this liberating way of life, presenting Shantideva's text verse by verse and offering both illuminating stories and practical exercises to enrich the text and bring its timeless teachings to life in our world today.

Comfortable with Uncertainty: 108 Teachings on Cultivating Fearlessness and Compassion

Collecting some of the most powerful passages from Pema Chödrön's many beloved books, this compact handbook for spiritual practice is rich with inspiration and insight. Here she explores life-changing concepts, themes, and practices from the Buddhist tradition, showing how anyone (not just Buddhists) can draw from them to become more courageous, aware, and kindhearted. It includes the benefits of meditation and mindfulness, letting go of the fixations that weigh us down, working directly with fear and other painful emotions, and much more.

The Compassion Book

Here Pema Chödrön introduces a powerful, transformative practice called *lojong*, which has been a primary focus of her teachings and personal practice for many years. This book presents fifty-nine pithy slogans from the *lojong* teachings for daily contemplation and includes Pema's clear, succinct guidance on how to understand them—and how they can enrich our lives. It also features a forty-five minute downloadable audio program titled "Opening the Heart."

Living Beautifully with Uncertainty and Change

We live in difficult times. Life sometimes seems like a roiling and turbulent river threatening to drown us and destroy the world. Why, then, shouldn't we cling to the certainty of the shore—to our familiar patterns and habits? Because, Pema Chödrön teaches, that kind of fear-based clinging keeps us from the infinitely more satisfying experience of being fully alive. The teachings she presents here—known as the "Three Commitments"—provide a wealth of wisdom for learning to step right into the river: to be completely, fearlessly present even in the hardest times, the most difficult situations.

The Places That Scare You: A Guide to Fearlessness in Difficult Times

We always have a choice in how we react to the circumstances of our lives. We can let them harden us and make us increasingly resentful and afraid, or we can let them soften us and allow our inherent human kindness to shine through. Here Pema Chödrön provides essential tools for dealing with the many difficulties that life throws our way, teaching us how to awaken our basic human goodness and connect deeply with others—to accept ourselves and everything around us complete with faults and imperfections. If we go to the places that scare us, Pema suggests, we just might find the boundless life we've always dreamed of.

The Pocket Pema Chödrön

This treasury of 108 short selections from the best-selling books of Pema Chödrön offers teachings on breaking free of destructive patterns; developing patience, kindness, and joy amid our everyday struggles; becoming fearless; and unlocking our natural warmth, intelligence, and goodness. Designed for on-the-go inspiration, this is a perfect guide to Buddhist principles and the foundations of meditation and mindfulness.

Practicing Peace

In this pocket-size guide to the practice of inner peace, Pema Chödrön shows us how to look deeply at the underlying causes of our tensions and how we really *can* create a more peaceful world—by starting right where we are and learning to see the seeds of hostility in our hearts. She draws on Buddhist teachings to explore the origins of anger, aggression, hatred, and war, and offers practical techniques all of us can use to work for genuine, lasting peace in our own lives and in whatever circumstances we find ourselves.

Start Where You Are: A Guide to Compassionate Living

Pema here offers down-to-earth guidance on how we can go beyond the fleeting attempts to "fix" our pain and, instead, take our lives as they are as the only path to achieve what we all yearn for most deeply—to embrace rather than deny the difficulties of our lives. These teachings, framed around the fifty-nine traditional Tibetan Buddhist maxims known as the *lojong* slogans—such as "Always meditate on whatever provokes resentment," "Be grateful to everyone," and "Don't expect applause"—point us directly to our own hearts and minds. By working with these slogans as everyday meditations, *Start Where You Are* shows how we can all develop the courage to work with our own inner pain and discover true joy, holistic well-being, and unshakeable confidence.

Taking the Leap: Freeing Ourselves from Old Habits and Fears

These classic Buddhist teachings about *shenpa* (painful attachments and compulsions) help us see how certain habits of mind tend to "hook" us and get us stuck in states of anger, blame, self-hatred, and addiction—and how we can liberate ourselves from them. Pema offers insights and practices we can immediately put to use in our lives to take a bold leap toward a new way of living—one that will bring about positive transformation for ourselves and for our troubled world.

When Things Fall Apart: Heart Advice for Difficult Times

How can we live our lives when everything seems to fall apart—when we are continually overcome by fear, anxiety, and pain? The answer, Pema Chödrön suggests, might be just the opposite of what you expect. Here, in her most beloved and acclaimed work, Pema shows that moving *toward* painful situations and becoming intimate with them can open up our hearts in ways we never before imagined. Drawing from traditional Buddhist wisdom, she offers life-changing tools for transforming suffering and negative patterns into habitual ease and boundless joy.

The Wisdom of No Escape: And the Path of Loving-Kindness

In this guide to true kindness for self and others, Pema Chödrön presents a uniquely practical approach to opening ourselves up to life in all circumstances. She reveals that when we embrace the happiness and heartache, inspiration and confusion, and all the twists and turns that are a natural part of life, we can begin to discover a true wellspring of courageous love that's been within our hearts all along.

AUDIO

Be Grateful to Everyone: An In-Depth Guide to the Practice of Lojong

One of the best ways to bring meditation off the cushion and into everyday life is to practice *lojong* (or mind training). For centuries, Tibetans have used fifty-nine powerful mind-training slogans as a way to transform life's ordinary situations into opportunities for awakening. Pema Chödrön here presents her definitive audio teachings on *lojong*. She offers an overview of the practice and goes on to provide inspiring commentary on the slogans while paying special attention to how to apply them on the spot in our daily lives.

Comfortable with Uncertainty: 108 Teachings on Cultivating Fearlessness and Compassion

This audiobook offers short, stand-alone teachings designed to help us cultivate compassion and awareness amid the challenges of daily living. More than a collection of thoughts for the day, *Comfortable with Uncertainty* offers a progressive program of spiritual study, leading the reader through essential concepts, themes, and practices on the Buddhist path.

Don't Bite the Hook: Finding Freedom from Anger, Resentment, and Other Destructive Emotions

In this recorded weekend retreat, Pema draws on Buddhist teachings to show us how to relate constructively to the inevitable shocks, losses, and frustrations of life so that we can find true happiness. The key, Pema explains, is not biting the "hook" of our habitual responses.

The Fearless Heart: The Practice of Living with Courage and Compassion

Pema shows us how to transform negative emotions like fear and guilt into courageous self-acceptance in *The Fearless Heart*. Her teachings are based on five aphorisms presented to Machik Lapdron, one of Tibetan Buddhism's greatest female teachers. Pema offers insightful guidance on how to remain courageous in the face of pain, and how to increase feelings of generosity and passion through fearlessness. This audio program includes an extensive question-and-answer session and guided meditation practices available for the first time.

Fully Alive: A Retreat with Pema Chödrön on Living Beautifully with Uncertainty and Change

In this recorded weekend retreat, Pema Chödrön and her teaching assistant, Meg Wheatley, teach us to stop clinging to the certainty of life's shore and to instead step right into the river: to be completely, fearlessly present, even in the hardest times, the most difficult situations. That's the secret of being fully alive.

Giving Our Best: A Retreat with Pema Chödrön on Practicing the Way of the Bodhisattva

Pema Chödrön here teaches on how to nurture a compassionate attitude, using a text that is very close to her heart: the Buddhist classic known as *The Way of the Bodhisattva*. She focuses on its primary subject, the enlightened heart and mind (*bodhichitta*), showing us how this awakened state, which often seems infinitely far out of our grasp, is always available to us right where we are.

Perfect Just as You Are: Buddhist Practices on the Four Limitless Ones—Loving-Kindness, Compassion, Joy, and Equanimity

Here are Pema Chödrön's definitive teachings on the Buddhist practice called the "Four Limitless Ones"—a practice that helps us recognize and grow the seeds of love, compassion, joy, and equanimity already present in our hearts. This in-depth study course offers guided meditations, on-the-spot practices to use in the midst of daily life, an overview of *bodhichitta* and the bodhisattva vow, guided shamatha meditation, writing and reflection exercises, methods to weaken the grip of negative emotions, and question-and-answer sessions.

Smile at Fear: A Retreat with Pema Chödrön on Discovering Your Radiant Self-Confidence

Behind each of our fears resides a basic fear of *ourselves*. In this recorded retreat, Pema Chödrön shares teachings inspired by the book *Smile at Fear*, which was written by her teacher Chögyam Trungpa. Here is a vision for moving beyond this most basic fear of self to discover the innate bravery, trust, and joy that reside at the core of our being.

Start Where You Are: A Guide to Compassionate Living

With insight and humor, Pema Chödrön offers guidance on how we can accept our flaws and embrace ourselves wholeheartedly as a prerequisite for developing compassion. Through working with fifty-nine Tibetan Buddhist *lojong* slogans, Pema shows us how to develop the courage to face our inner pain and thereby discover a wealth of freedom, well-being, and confidence.

This Moment Is the Perfect Teacher: Ten Buddhist Teachings on Cultivating Inner Strength and Compassion

Lojong is a powerful Tibetan Buddhist practice created especially for training the mind to work with the challenges of everyday living. It teaches our hearts to soften, reframes our attitude toward difficulty, and allows us to discover a wellspring of inner strength. In this recorded retreat, Pema Chödrön introduces the *lojong* teachings and explains how we can apply them to any situation in our life—because, as Pema says, "every moment is an opportunity for awakening."

When Things Fall Apart: Heart Advice for Difficult Times

This abridged audiobook based on the beloved spiritual classic contains radical and compassionate advice for what to do when our lives become painful and difficult. Read by Pema, it includes instructions on how to use painful emotions to cultivate wisdom, compassion, and courage; how to communicate in a way that leads to openness and true intimacy with others; and how to reverse negative habitual patterns.

The Wisdom of No Escape: And the Path of Loving-Kindness

It's true, as they say, that we can love others only when we first love ourselves, and we can experience real joy only when we stop running from pain. The key to understanding these truisms lies in remaining open to life in all circumstances, and here Pema Chödrön shows us how.